SUMANA RAY

INDIAN VEGETARIAN COOKING

SUMANA RAY

INDIAN VEGETARIAN COOKING

CHARTWELL BOOKS, INC.

Cabbage
Pumpkin
Spinach
Doddy
Cauliflower
White raddish
Tomatoes
Coriander leaves
Bitter gourd
Green pepper
Beans
Aubergine
Mushrooms
White raddish
Okra

A QUINTET BOOK

Published by Chartwell Books Inc.,
A Division of Book Sales Inc.,
110 Enterprise Avenue,
Secaucus, New Jersey 07094

ISBN 0-89009-830-1

This book was designed and produced by Quintet Publishing Limited 32 Kingly Court, London W1

Art Design Bridgewater Associates
Illustrator Lorraine Harrison
Photographer Michael Freeman
Editor Cheen Horn

Typeset in Great Britain by Leaper and Gard Limited, Bristol
Color Origination in Hong Kong by Hong Kong Graphic Arts Limited
Printed in Hong Kong by Leefung-Asco Printers Limited

Indian vegetarian cookery has survived through the span of seven hundred years of foreign rule.

Whereas influences from the Mughals, Portuguese, Persians and the British undoubtedly created many new ideas in the non-vegetarian cuisine, they made little difference, if any, in terms of evolution of the vegetarian style of cooking.

Probably an outstanding reason for this influence, or the lack of it, was the caste system, in which the Brahmins – the monitors of the Hindu faith and its temples – were entrusted with the entire wealth of the other castes of the Hindu religion.

The Brahmins taught 'ahimsa' – non-violence – and the avoidance of the eating of meat. They were successful in building barriers between the Mughal rulers and their Hindu subjects by making the cow, which the Mughals ate, a sacred animal that their subjects were prohibited from eating.

Added to these essential political factors, climatic and economic factors contributed to the development of Indian vegetarian cooking as we know it today. Firstly, due to the tropical climate in most areas of India, meat deteriorates extremely fast and, secondly, by growing vegetables the Hindus could live off the land easily, making themselves completely self-sufficient.

All those reasons have become into one predominant view: that Indians eat vegetarian food because of their religious beliefs.

The Indian sub-continent is a huge land mass that supports an astonishing diversity of peoples – there are fourteen major languages and about a hundred dialects. Its cuisine is correspondingly varied, and it is impossible to represent it in its entirety; all one can say is that, as a general rule, food is inclined to be hotter the further south its origin. I have chosen an extremely simple approach to suit anyone living outside India who is nevertheless interested enough to cook their own Indian food.

Years ago, there were no cookery books and young Indian girls learned from their mothers and their elders in the family. The elders would simply mention the ingredients for a particular dish and the young girl had to keep on experimenting to achieve perfection. I have added the quantity of spices that suit my family and friends, but you can always increase or decrease the quantity of spices to suit your individual taste.

Most of my cooking has been done using one utensil which is called a 'karai', quite similar to the Chinese 'wok'. The main aim is to use as little oil as possible; bearing this in mind, a saucepan or a frying pan would serve just as well.

All my recipes are presented in a very simple way, and I do hope you enjoy this book.

Sumana Ray

Asafetida (Hing)
A strong aromatic resin, available in powdered form. Has a pungent flavour.

Cardamom (Elaichi)
These pods are whitish or light green in colour. They are the most important ingredient in the preparation of Garam Masala. They can be used whole or the seeds can be ground. When used whole, make sure that the skin is broken, allowing the flavour to escape.

Chilli (Mirchi)
Dried chillies can be used whole or ground. Add very sparingly to curries to enhance the flavour and make the preparation hot. Go easy on the chilli seeds as they contain the vital 'hot' quality.

Cinnamon (Dalchini)
Used mainly to accentuate the rich aroma and to add a full flavour to the preparation.

Coriander (Dhaniya)
Tiny round aromatic seeds, usually ground to yield best results.

Coriander Leaves
These are used for garnishing or added towards the end of the preparation. They are a very versatile ingredient and can be used in almost any recipe.

Cumin (Jeera)
A common ingredient in Indian recipes. It can be used whole, ground, or roasted and then ground.

Curry Leaves
Used a great deal in South Indian dishes for flavouring. Can be bought fresh or dried.

Dried Mango Powder (Amchoor)
Used mainly to bring out the flavour of particular preparations and the taste is definitely sour.

Fennel (Sounf)
Small oval-shaped pale green seeds which have digestive properties. Has a close resemblance in taste to aniseed. Sometimes used in the preparation of curries.

Fenugreek (Methi)
The seeds are an orange-ish brown in colour and have a slightly bitter after-taste.

Mustard (Rai)
Available in two forms: leaves (which can be cooked like spinach); and tiny reddish-brown seeds which can be used whole or ground.

Onion Seeds (Kalonji)
Round black seeds almost always used whole.

Panch Phoron
This is a combination of five spices in equal proportions: cumin, kalonji, fennel, fenugreek and mustard. This combination is used for daals – lentils or vegetable preparations – and these spices should be used whole and not ground.

Poppy Seeds (Khus Khus)
Tiny round whitish seeds which can be ground to give preparations more consistency.

Tumeric (Haldi)
A member of the ginger family. In India the root is crushed to make haldi. However, this is difficult to find elsewhere. The best solution is to buy tumeric powder. This spice is used mainly for colouring and gives a lovely yellowish colour to curries.

All these spices are available at Indian grocery shops

Coriander Powder
Cardamom
Dried Chillis
Poppy Seed
Mustard Seed
Mustard
Onion Seed
Bay
Coriander Seed
Hing
Cumin
Cumin Powder
Tumeric
Chilli Powder
Methi
Cinnamon

EQUIPMENT

Chopping board
Knives
Food processor
Garlic crusher
Grater and peeler

Tongs
Rolling pin
Spatula
Karai
Saucepan & lid
Frying pan
Sieve

SIMPLE LUNCH OR DINNER 1

Rice with lentils
Spinach with lentils and vegetables
Vegetable fritters
Yoghurt
Papadums
Fritters in syrup

SIMPLE LUNCH OR DINNER 2

Stuffed deep fried bread 2
Potato curry
Pineapple chutney
Rice pudding

INFORMAL LUNCH OR DINNER 1

Pea pillau
Red lentils with fried onions
Vegetable cutlets
Aubergine with mustard
Potatoes with tamarind
Tomato cucumber and onion relish
Sandesh

INFORMAL LUNCH OR DINNER 2

Batora
Soured chickpeas
Spinach with cottage cheese
Yoghurt with aubergine
Carrot halva

FORMAL LUNCH OR DINNER 1

Pillau with coconut and milk
Wholewheat flat bread
Black eyed beans with onions
Mushrooms with potatoes and onions
Aubergines with sour cream
Cottage cheese with peas
Egg curry
Yoghurt with Boondi
Baked yoghurt
Carrot halva

FORMAL LUNCH OR DINNER 2

Fried rice
Roasted cauliflower
Potatoes with tamarind
Fried egg curry
Yoghurt with cucumber
Cheese balls in syrup
Yoghurt with saffron

FORMAL LUNCH OR DINNER 3

Plain Rice
Deep fried white bread
Channa dal
Panir bhujia
Dry potatoes
Spicy aubergine
Tomato chutney
Khir with oranges
Fritters in syrup

Each recipe serves 4–6 people but do bear in mind that with Indian food it is customary to serve several dishes rather than just one to make a complete meal.

These recipes are extremely versatile. They are ideal for picnics as they can be eaten cold, served with a salad or chutney. They can also be served as a side dish with a main course, or alternatively, as an hors d'oeuvre.

ALOO KABLI / SAVOURY POTATO SNACK

12 oz / 325 g / 3 cups potatoes, boiled and peeled
1 small onion, finely chopped
1-2 green chillis, finely chopped
½ tsp salt
½ tsp chilli powder
5-6 tbsp tamarind juice (see basic recipes)
1 tbsp coriander leaves, chopped

1 Cut the potatoes into ¼in / 5 cm slices and cool thoroughly.

2 Gently mix in all the other ingredients. Serve cold.

PANIR CUTLET / CHEESE CUTLET

- 1 tbsp ghee (see basic recipes)
- 8 fl oz / 225 ml / 1 cup milk
- 6 oz / 175 g / 1 cup panir (see basic recipes), drained
- 4 oz / 100 g / ⅔ cup semolina
- 1 medium onion, finely chopped
- 2 green chillis, finely chopped
- 1 tbsp coriander leaves, chopped
- ½ tsp salt
- 2 tbsp flour
- 4 fl oz / 100 ml / ½ cup milk
- breadcrumbs
- oil for deep frying

1 Heat the ghee in a karai over medium heat, add the milk, panir, semolina, onions, chilli, coriander leaves and salt and mix thoroughly. Stirring constantly, cook until the mixture leaves the sides and a ball forms, about 3-4 minutes.

2 Spread the mixture ¾ in / 1.5 cm on a greased baking tin. Cut into 1 in / 2.5 cm squares and chill for about 2 hours.

3 Make a smooth batter with the flour and milk. Dip each square in the batter and then roll it in breadcrumbs.

4 Heat the oil in a karai over high heat and fry the cutlets for 2-3 minutes till crisp and golden. Serve with chutney.

NIMKI / DEEP FRIED PASTRY

4 oz / 100 g / 1 cup flour
½ tsp salt
pinch of kalonji
pinch of ground roasted cumin (see basic recipes)
1½ tbsp oil
approx. 2 fl oz / 50 ml / ¼ cup hot water
oil for deep frying

1 Sieve the flour and salt together. Mix in the kalonji and cumin. Rub in the 1½ tbsp oil.

2 Add enough water to make a stiff dough. Knead for 10 minutes until soft and smooth.

3 Divide the dough into 12 balls. Roll each ball into thin rounds 4 in / 10 cm across. Make 5 or 6 small cuts in the rounds.

4 Heat oil in a karai over medium heat. Add a nimki and fry until crisp and golden. Drain on paper towels. Serve with chutney or dry potatoes (see page 71).

PAKORAS / VEGETABLE FRITTERS

Batter:
4 tbsp gram (chick pea) flour
2 tsp oil
1 tsp baking powder
½ tsp salt
3 oz / 75 ml / ⅜ cup water
Any of the following vegetables can be used:
aubergines (eggplant), cut into very thin rounds
onions, cut into ⅛ in / .25 cm rings
potatoes, cut into very thin rounds
cauliflower, cut into ¾ in / 1.5 cm florets
chilli, left whole
pumpkin, cut into thin slices
green pepper, cut into thin strips
oil for deep frying

1 Mix all the batter ingredients together and beat until smooth.

2 Wash the slices of vegetables and pat dry.

3 Heat the oil in a karai till very hot.

4 Dip a slice of the vegetable in the batter and put into the hot oil. Place as many slices as you can in the oil. Fry till crisp and golden. Drain and serve with mint or coriander chutney.

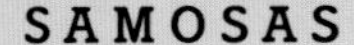

SAMOSAS

Filling:
3 tbsp oil
¼ tsp whole cumin seeds
1 lb / 450 g / 4 cups potatoes, diced into ½ in / 1 cm cubes
1 green chilli, finely chopped
pinch of turmeric
½ tsp salt
3 oz / 75 g / scant ½ cup peas
1 tsp ground roasted cumin (see basic recipes)
Dough:
8 oz / 225 g / 2¼ cups plain flour
1 tsp salt
3 tbsp oil
approx 3½ fl oz / 90 ml / scant ½ cup hot water
oil for deep frying

FILLING:

1 Heat the oil in a karai over medium high heat and add the cumin seeds. Let them sizzle for a few seconds.

2 Add the potatoes and green chilli and fry for 2-3 minutes. Add the turmeric and salt and, stirring occasionally, cook for 5 minutes.

3 Add the peas and the ground roasted cumin. Stir to mix. Cover, lower heat and cook a further 10 minutes until the potatoes are tender. Cool.

DOUGH:

1 Sieve together the flour and salt. Rub in the oil. Add enough water to form a stiff dough. Knead for 10 minutes until smooth.

2 Divide into 12 balls. Roll each ball into a round of about 6 in / 15 cm across. Cut in half.

3 Pick up one half, flatten it slightly and form a cone, sealing the overlapping edge with a little water. Fill the cone with 1½ tsp of the filling and seal the top with a little water.

4 In a similar way make all the samosas.

5 Heat oil in a karai over medium heat. Put in as many samosas as you can into the hot oil and fry until crisp and golden. Drain. Serve with a chutney.

DAHI VADA / LENTIL CAKES IN YOGHURT

8 oz / 225 g / 0 cups washed urid dal

15 fl oz / 425 ml / scant 2 cups water

3 green chillis

½ tsp salt

¼ tsp asafetida

oil for deep frying

1½ pints / 850 ml / 3¾ cups plain yoghurt

1 tsp ground roasted cumin (see basic recipes)

¼ tsp garam masala (see basic recipes)

½ tsp chilli powder

1 Wash the dal and soak in the water overnight.

2 In a liquidizer or a food processor put in the dal, green chillis, salt and asafetida and some of the soaking liquid. Blend until you have a thick paste, adding more soaking liquid as necessary.

3 In a karai heat the oil over medium high heat.

4 Add tablespoons of the mixture to the hot oil and fry for 3-4 minutes, until they are reddish brown, turning once. Drain them on paper towels.

5 When all the vadas are fried put them in a bowl of warm water for 1 minute. Squeeze out the water gently and put in a large dish.

6 Combine the yoghurt, roasted cumin, garam masala and chilli powder and pour over the vadas.

7 Chill and serve with tamarind chutney (see chutneys).

ALOO TIKKA / FRIED POTATO CAKES

1 lb / 450 g / 5 cups potatoes, boiled and mashed

1-2 green chillis, chopped

½ tsp salt

1 tbsp coriander leaves, chopped

2 tbsp onions, chopped

oil for frying

1 Mix the mashed potatoes with the chillis, salt, coriander leaves and onions.

2 Form into small balls and flatten.

3 Heat oil for shallow frying till hot and fry the potato cakes for a few minutes each side till golden. Serve with a chutney.

KELA KOFTA / GREEN BANANA BALLS

1 green banana, cut in half
1 green chilli, chopped
½ tbsp coriander leaves, chopped
½ tsp salt
1 tbsp onion, chopped
1 tsp plain flour
oil for deep frying

1 Boil the banana till soft. Peel and cool.

2 Mash the banana with the chilli, coriander leaves, salt, onion and flour. Divide the mixture into 8 small balls and flatten.

3 Heat the oil and fry the koftas, turning once, till crisp and golden.

SABZI CUTLET / VEGETABLE CUTLET

4 oz / 100 g / 1 cup beetroot, diced
4 oz / 100 g / 1 cup carrots, diced
8 oz / 225 g / 2 cups potatoes, diced
4 oz / 100 g / 1½ cups cabbage, shredded
½ tsp chilli powder
½ tsp ground roasted cumin (see basic recipes)
½ tsp ground black pepper
¾ tsp salt
a big pinch sugar
1 tbsp raisins (optional)
2 oz / 50 g / ½ cup flour
4 oz / 100 ml / ½ cup milk
breadcrumbs
oil for deep frying

1 Boil the beetroot, carrots, potatoes and cabbage together until tender. Drain.

2 Mash the boiled vegetables with the chilli, roasted cumin, black pepper, salt, sugar and raisins. Divide into 12 balls and flatten. Chill for 1 hour.

3 Make a batter with the flour and milk and dip a cutlet in it. Then roll it in breadcrumbs until well coated.

4 Heat the oil in a large frying pan and fry the cutlets for 2-3 minutes turning once, until crisp and golden. Serve with coriander chutney (see chutneys).

EGGS

OMELETTE CURRY

6 eggs
½ tsp salt
6 tbsp oil
1 large potato, cut into 1 in / 2.5 cm pieces
4 tbsp onion mixture (see basic recipes)
1 tsp ground turmeric
½ tsp chilli powder
¾ tsp salt
12 fl oz / 325 ml / 1½ cups water

1 Whisk the eggs and the salt together.

2 Heat 1 tbsp of the oil in a large frying pan and make an omelette with half the beaten eggs. Set aside and cut into four pieces. Similarly, make another omelette.

3 Heat the rest of the oil and fry the potatoes until lightly browned. Set aside. Add the onion mixture and fry for 2-3 minutes. Add the turmeric, chilli, and salt and stir well with the onion mixture.

4 Add the water and bring it to boil. Put in the potatoes, cover, lower heat and simmer for 10 minutes. Place the pieces of omelette in the pan, cover again and cook until the potatoes are tender, about another 10 minutes.

UNDEY KA DEVIL / DEVILLED EGGS

4 hard-boiled eggs, cut in half – lengthwise
1½ tbsp onions, finely chopped
2 green chillis, finely chopped
1 tbsp coriander leaves, chopped
½ tsp salt
2 tbsp mashed potatoes
oil for deep frying
1 tbsp plain flour
2 fl oz / 50 ml / ¼ cup water

1 Remove the yolks and mix with the onions, chillis, coriander leaves, salt and mashed potatoes. Put the mixture back into the egg whites. Chill for 30 minutes.

2 Heat the oil in a karai over high heat. While the oil is heating up make a batter with the flour and water. Be careful not to allow the oil to catch fire.

3 Dip eggs into the batter and gently put into the hot oil. Fry until golden, turning once.

UNDEY KI CURRY / EGG CURRY

4 tbsp oil
1 large onion, finely sliced
2 tbsp onion mixture (see basic recipes)
½ tsp ground turmeric
½ tsp chilli powder
¾ tsp salt
a big pinch of sugar
8 hard-boiled eggs
4 fl oz / 100 ml / ½ cup water

1 Heat the oil in a frying pan over medium high heat and fry the sliced onion for 3-4 minutes until lightly browned.

2 Add the onion mixture, turmeric, chilli, salt and sugar and, stirring constantly, fry for another 2-3 minutes. Add the eggs and mix until well covered with the spices.

3 Add the water, bring it to the boil, lower heat, cover and cook for about 10 minutes until the gravy thickens.

MASALA UNDEY / FRIED EGG CURRY

- 3 medium onions
- 5 cloves garlic
- 1 inch / 2.5 cm root ginger
- 1 tbsp white vinegar
- 8 tbsp mustard oil
- 8 eggs
- 3 bay leaves
- 2 inch / 5 cm stick cinnamon
- 6 cardamoms
- 2-3 green chillis
- 1½ tsp ground turmeric
- ½ tsp chilli powder
- 1 tsp salt
- ¼ tsp sugar

1 Blend the onions, garlic, ginger and vinegar in a blender until you have a fine paste.

2 Heat the oil in a large frying pan over a medium heat, fry the eggs one at a time and set aside.

3 To the remaining oil add the bay leaves, cinnamon and cardamoms and let them sizzle for a few seconds.

4 Add the blended paste and the green chillis and fry for 6-8 minutes, stirring constantly. Add the turmeric, chilli powder, salt and sugar and continue frying for another minute.

5 Carefully add the eggs and, stirring gently, cover them with some of the spices.

6 Cover and cook for 5 minutes. Serve hot with a pillau (see rice dishes).

Moong Dal
Split yellow bean, cleaned of husk.
Chole (Chickpeas)
Rounded, beige unsplit peas.
Musoor Dal (Split Red Lentils)
Pink in colour, cook easily.
Channa Dal
Smaller in size than split peas,
yellow in colour.
Rajma (Red Kidney Beans)
Cook more easily if soaked
overnight first.
Lobia (Black Eyed Beans)
Small beige beans with a black dot.
Have a smoky flavour.
Urid Dal (Dehulled Split Matpe)
Small whitish lentil.
Matar Dal (Split Peas)
Round yellow lentils, uniform in size.

As they are very rich in protein, pulses are a staple diet for vegetarians. Some types of pulse have to be soaked overnight so that they remain tender after cooking. They can be served with rice or bread and most types of vegetarian food.

CHANNA DAL

- 7 oz / 200 g / scant 1 cup channa dal, washed
- 2½ pints / 1.4 litres / 6¼ cups water
- 1½ tbsp ghee (see basic recipes)
- ¾ tsp whole cumin seeds
- 2 bay leaves
- 2 dried red chillis
- 2 inch / 5 cm cinnamon stick
- 4 cardamoms
- ¾ tsp ground turmeric
- ½ tsp chilli powder
- 1¼ tsp ground cumin
- 1 tsp salt
- ½ tsp sugar
- 2 tbsp dessicated coconut
- 1 tbsp raisins

1 Bring the dal and water to the boil in a large saucepan over medium high heat. Skim off any scum that forms.

2 Lower the heat, partially cover the pan and simmer for about 1 hour 15 minutes until soft.

3 Heat ghee in a small pan over medium heat, add the whole cumin seeds, bay leaves, red chillis, cinnamon stick and cardamoms and let them sizzle for a few seconds.

4 Add the turmeric, chilli powder, ground cumin, salt and sugar and stir fry for 1 minute. Add the dessicated coconut and raisins and fry for another 1-2 minutes.

5 Mix the ghee and spices with the dal and stir. Serve with rice or lucchi (see bread) and aloo dam (see page 66).

MOONG DAL

7 oz / 200 g / scant 1 cup moong dal
2½ pints / 1.4 litres / 5 cups water
¼ tsp ground turmeric
1 tsp ground cumin
2 tomatoes, chopped
1 tsp salt
1 tbsp ghee (see basic recipes)
¾ tsp whole cumin seeds
2 dried red chillis
2 bay leaves
1 inch / 2.5 cm cinnamon stick
4 cardamoms

1 Heat a saucepan and dry roast the lentils stirring constantly until all the lentils turn light brown.

2 Wash the lentils in several changes of water and bring to boil in the measured amount of water in a large saucepan. Skim off any scum that forms.

3 Lower the heat, add the turmeric, cumin, tomatoes and salt and partially cover and simmer for about 1 hour 15 minutes until the lentils are soft.

4 In a small pan heat the ghee over medium heat, add the cumin seeds, red chillis, bay leaves, cinnamon stick and cardamoms and let them sizzle for a few seconds.

5 Add the hot ghee and spices to the lentils and stir. Serve with rice.

MUSOOR DAL / RED LENTILS WITH FRIED ONIONS

7 oz / 200 g / scant cup red lentils, washed
1¾ pints / 1 litre / 4⅜ cups water
¼ tsp ground turmeric
1½ tsp ground cumin
2 tomatoes, chopped
½ tsp salt
2-3 green chillies
1 tbsp coriander leaves, chopped
3 tbsp ghee (see basic recipes)
3 cloves garlic, crushed
1 onion, finely sliced

1 Bring the lentils to the boil in the measured amount of water in a large saucepan. Remove any scum that forms.

2 Add the turmeric, cumin and tomatoes, and mix with the lentils.

3 Lower the heat, partially cover and simmer the lentils for about 40 minutes until tender. Add the salt, chillis and coriander leaves and mix in with the lentils. Remove from the heat.

4 In a small pan, heat the ghee. Add the garlic and onion and fry until golden brown.

5 Pour over the lentils and serve with rice.

DAL TARKARI / SPLIT PEAS WITH VEGETABLES

7 oz / 200 g / scant cup split peas, washed
25 fl oz / 700 ml / 3 cups water
2 tbsp ghee (see basic recipes)
½ tsp whole cumin seeds
2 bay leaves
2-3 green chillis, cut lengthwise
10 oz / 275 g / 2½ cups potatoes, cut into 1 in / 2.5 cm pieces
3 oz / 75 g / ⅓ cup peas
12 oz / 350 g / 3 cups cauliflower, cut into large florets
½ tsp ground turmeric
1 tsp salt

1 In a large saucepan bring the split peas and water to the boil. Cover and simmer for 30 minutes. Remove from heat.

2 Heat the ghee in a large saucepan over medium high heat. Add the cumin seeds, bay leaves and green chillis and let them sizzle for a few seconds.

3 Add the potatoes, peas, cauliflower and fry for 1-2 minutes.

4 Add the boiled split peas with the water, turmeric and salt. Mix thoroughly, lower heat and cook until the vegetables are tender. (If the dal gets too thick add a little more water.)

LOBIA AUR PYAZ / BLACK EYE PEAS WITH ONIONS

7 oz / 200 g / generous cup black eye beans, washed
2 pints / 1.1 litres / 5 cups water
2 tbsp oil
1 large onion, finely chopped
2 cloves garlic, crushed
¼ in / 0.5 cm root ginger, grated
1-2 green chillis, finely chopped
½ tsp salt
1 tsp molasses

1 Soak the beans in the water overnight.

2 Boil the beans in the water and then cover and simmer for 1 hour until tender. Drain.

3 Heat the oil in a large saucepan and fry the onion, garlic, ginger and chilli until the onions are soft.

4 Add the beans, salt and molasses and cook until all the moisture is absorbed, about 15 minutes. Serve with chappatis (see bread).

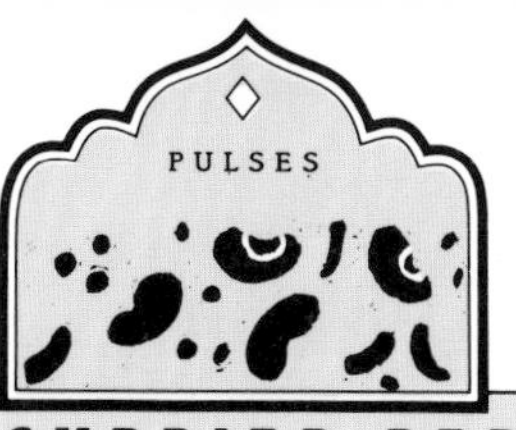

MASALA RAJMA/CURRIED RED KIDNEY BEANS

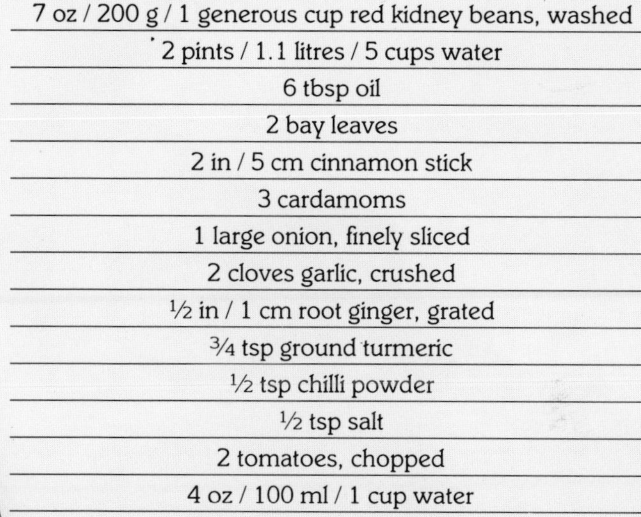

7 oz / 200 g / 1 generous cup red kidney beans, washed
2 pints / 1.1 litres / 5 cups water
6 tbsp oil
2 bay leaves
2 in / 5 cm cinnamon stick
3 cardamoms
1 large onion, finely sliced
2 cloves garlic, crushed
½ in / 1 cm root ginger, grated
¾ tsp ground turmeric
½ tsp chilli powder
½ tsp salt
2 tomatoes, chopped
4 oz / 100 ml / 1 cup water

1 Soak the beans in the water overnight.

2 Boil the beans in the water and then cover and simmer for 1 hour until tender. Drain.

3 Heat the oil in a large saucepan over medium high heat and put in the bay leaves, cinnamon and cardamoms and let them sizzle for a few seconds. Add the onion, garlic and ginger and fry until the onions are golden brown.

4 Add the turmeric, chilli, salt and tomatoes and fry for 1 minute. Add the drained beans and fry with the spices for 2-3 minutes.

5 Add 4 oz / 100 ml / 1 cup water and bring to the boil, stirring occasionally. Cover, lower heat and cook for 10-15 minutes. Serve with chappatis (see bread).

KABLI CHANNA/CURRIED CHICK PEAS

- 7 oz / 200 g / generous cup chick peas, washed
- 1½ pints / 825 ml / 3¾ cups water
- 4 tbsp oil
- pinch of asafetida
- ½ tsp whole cumin seeds
- ½ tsp ground turmeric
- ½ tsp chilli powder
- 1 tsp ground coriander
- 1 tsp ground cumin
- 1½ tsp amchoor
- ½ tsp salt
- 2 tbsp lemon juice
- 1 tbsp coriander leaves, chopped
- 1-2 green chillis, chopped

1 Soak the chick peas in the water overnight.

2 Boil the chick peas with the water, cover and simmer for about 1 hour until tender. Drain and save the liquid.

3 Heat the oil in a large saucepan over medium heat and add the asafetida and cumin seeds. Let them sizzle for a few seconds.

4 Add the drained chickpeas, turmeric, chilli powder, coriander, cumin, amchoor and salt and stir fry for 2-3 minutes.

5 Add 8 fl oz / 225 ml / 1 cup of the chick pea stock and cook for 20 minutes, stirring occasionally.

6 Before serving sprinkle with the lemon juice, coriander leaves and green chillis. Serve with batora (see page 94).

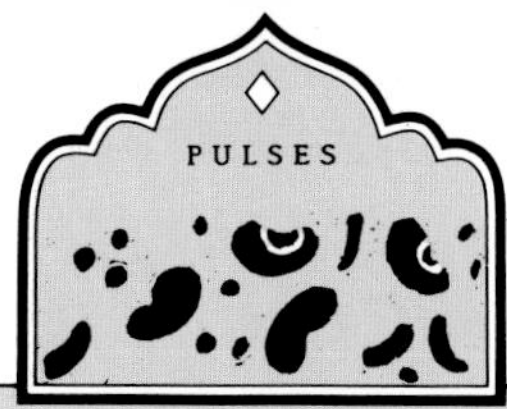

CHOLE / SOURED CHICK PEAS

7 oz / 200 g / generous cup chick peas, washed
1½ pints / 825 ml / 3¾ cups water
1 teabag
3 tbsp oil
8 oz / 225 g / 2 cups potatoes, boiled and diced into ½ in / 1 cm cubes
2 medium onions, finely chopped
1 clove garlic, crushed
½ in / 1 cm root ginger, grated
2 tsp ground coriander
2 green chillis, chopped
1½ tbsp amchoor
½ tsp chilli powder
¾ tsp salt
6 fl oz / 175 ml / ¾ cup water
1½ tsp garam masala (see basic recipes)

1 Soak the chick peas in the water with the teabag overnight.

2 Discard the teabag and place the chickpeas and the water in a saucepan and bring to boil. Cover and simmer for about 1 hour until tender. Drain.

3 Heat the oil in a saucepan over medium heat and fry the diced potatoes until lightly browned. Set aside.

4 In the remaining oil fry the onions until golden brown. Add the garlic and ginger and fry a further 2 minutes.

5 Add the chickpeas, coriander, green chillis, amchoor, chilli, salt and potatoes and stir fry for about 2 minutes until well mixed.

6 Add the water and cook for about 15 minutes. Sprinkle with garam masala. Serve hot with batora (see page 94).

VEGETABLES

BUND GOBI KI ROLLS / CABBAGE ROLLS

- 8 large cabbage leaves, parboiled for 5 minutes and drained
- 3 tbsp oil
- 2 medium onions, finely chopped
- 7 oz / 200 g / generous 1 cup panir (see basic recipes), drained
- ½ tsp ground turmeric
- ½ tsp chilli powder
- ½ tsp garam masala (see basic recipes)
- 1-2 green chillis, chopped
- ½ tsp salt
- 1 tbsp coriander leaves, chopped
- string for tying rolls
- oil for shallow frying

1 Heat the 3 tablespoons of oil in a frying pan over medium high heat and fry the onions till lightly browned.

2 Add the panir, turmeric, chilli, garam masala, green chillis, and salt and stir fry for 5-6 minutes. Sprinkle with the coriander leaves and remove from the heat.

3 Place 2 tablespoons of the mixture on a cabbage leaf and roll up, folding the two sides in. Tie with the string. Make all the rolls in the same way.

4 Heat oil for shallow frying over medium heat and fry the rolls, turning once, till browned.

BUND GOBI AUR NAZIAL / CABBAGE WITH COCONUT

2 tbsp oil
2 bay leaves
¾ tsp whole cumin seeds
1-2 green chillis, chopped
1½ lbs / 700 g / 9 cups cabbage, shredded
¾ tsp salt
⅓ tsp sugar
3 tbsp dessicated coconut
½ tsp ground cumin

1 Heat oil in a karai over medium high heat and add the bay leaves, cumin seeds and the green chillis and let them sizzle for a few seconds.

2 Add the cabbage, salt and sugar and mix. Cover, lower heat to medium and cook for about 15 minutes until half done.

3 Add the coconut and ground cumin and fry, stirring constantly for 10-15 minutes until all the moisture has evaporated.

MOOLI / WHITE RADISH

2 tbsp oil
½ tsp kalonji
1-2 green chillis, chopped
1 lb / 450 g / 4 cups white radish, peeled and grated
½ tsp salt
¼ tsp sugar

1 Heat the oil in a karai, add the kalonji and green chillis and let them sizzle for a few seconds.

2 Add the radish and stir fry for 2-3 minutes. Cover, lower the heat and cook for about 15 minutes, stirring occasionally.

3 Add the salt and sugar, increase the heat to medium high and, stirring constantly, cook till dry and brown.

BUND GOBI AUR MATER / CABBAGE WITH PEAS

3 tbsp oil
2 bay leaves
¾ tsp whole cumin seeds
1½ lb / 700 g / 9 cups cabbage, finely shredded
1 tsp ground turmeric
½ tsp chilli powder
1½ tsp ground cumin
1 tsp ground coriander
2 tomatoes, chopped
¾ tsp salt
½ tsp sugar
4 oz / 100 g / ½ cup peas

1 Heat the oil in a karai over medium high heat and add the bay leaves and the cumin seeds. Let them sizzle for a few seconds.

2 Add the cabbage and stir for 2-3 minutes.

3 Add the turmeric, chilli, cumin, coriander, tomatoes, salt and sugar and mix with the cabbage.

4 Lower heat, cover and cook for 15 minutes. Add the peas and cover again. Continue to cook for a further 15 minutes, stirring occasionally.

5 Remove the cover, turn heat up to medium high and, stirring continuously, cook until it is dry.

BHINDI BHAJI / FRIED OKRA WITH ONIONS

1 lb / 450 g okra
3 tbsp oil
2 large onions, finely chopped
1 tsp salt

1 Wash the okra and pat dry with paper towels.

2 Cut into ½ inch / 1 cm pieces.

3 Heat oil in a karai over medium heat and fry the onions until soft.

4 Add the okra and salt, and, stirring gently, continue frying until the okra is cooked, about 10-12 minutes. Serve with rice and lentils or paratha (see bread).

SARSO BHINDI / OKRA WITH MUSTARD

1½ tsp ground mustard
½ tsp ground turmeric
¼ tsp chilli powder
¾ tsp salt
2 tbsp hot water
1 lb / 450 g okra
4 tbsp oil
½ tsp kalonji
2-3 green chillis, cut lengthwise
1½ tbsp yoghurt
3 fl oz / 75 ml / ⅜ cups water

1 Mix the mustard, turmeric, chilli and salt with the hot water, cover and set aside 20 minutes.

2 Wash the okra, pat dry with paper towels. Cut off the tops and leave whole.

3 Heat oil in a karai over medium high heat, add the kalonji and green chillis and let them sizzle for a few seconds.

4 Add the okra and, stirring gently, fry for 5 minutes.

5 Add the spice mixture and yoghurt and mix with the okra; add the water and bring it to boil. Lower heat, cover and simmer till the okra is tender.

SAI BHAJI / SPINACH WITH LENTILS AND VEGETABLES

2 oz / 50 g / ¼ cup channa dal, washed
20 fl oz / 550 ml / 2½ cups water
3 tbsp oil
1 medium onion, finely chopped
½ in / 1 cm root ginger, grated
2 cloves garlic, crushed
9 oz / 250 g / ½ cup spinach, washed and chopped
1 medium potato, diced into ½ in / 1 cm cubes
3 tomatoes, chopped
2 oz / 50 g / ¼ cup peas
½ tsp ground turmeric
½ tsp chilli powder
1 tsp ground coriander
½ tsp salt

1 Bring the dal to the boil in the water over high heat. Cover and simmer for about 40 minutes until the dal is tender. Drain and save the liquid; make it up to 12 fl oz / 325 ml / 1½ cups with water, if necessary.

2 Heat the oil in a large saucepan over medium high heat and fry the onion, ginger and garlic until soft.

3 Add the cooked dal and the rest of the ingredients and stir fry for 2-3 minutes. Add the liquid, cover, lower heat to medium low and cook for about 30 minutes.

TEL BAIGAN / MASALA AUBERGINE (EGGPLANT)

1 large aubergine, cut into large pieces
½ tsp salt
big pinch of turmeric
8 tbsp mustard oil
½ tsp kalonji
¾ tsp ground turmeric
½ tsp chilli powder
½ tsp salt
¼ tsp sugar
4 tbsp yoghurt
2 fl oz / 50 ml / ¼ cup water
2-3 green chillis
1 tsp ground roasted cumin (see basic recipes)

1 Rub the aubergine pieces with the ½ tsp salt and a big pinch of turmeric and set aside for 30 minutes.

2 Heat the oil in a karai over high heat and fry the aubergines until brown. Drain on paper towels.

3 Lower the heat to medium and add the kalonji. After 4-5 seconds add the turmeric, chilli powder, salt, sugar and yoghurt. Stir fry for 1 minute.

4 Add the water; when it starts to boil add the aubergines and green chillis and cook for 5 minutes.

5 Before removing from the heat sprinkle with the ground roasted cumin. Serve with rice.

DAHI BHINDI / OKRA WITH YOGHURT

- 1 lb / 450 g okra
- 4 tbsp oil
- ½ tsp panch phoron
- ½ in / 1 cm root ginger, grated
- 2 green chillis, cut lengthwise
- Big pinch of turmeric
- ½ tsp salt
- 5 fl oz / 125 ml / ⅝ cups yoghurt
- 8-10 curry leaves

1 Wash the okra and pat dry on kitchen towels. Cut into 1 in / 2.5 cm pieces.

2 Heat oil in a karai over medium high heat, add the panch phoron, ginger and chillis. Let them sizzle for a few seconds.

3 Add the okra, and stirring gently fry for 5 minutes. Lower heat to medium low.

4 Add the turmeric, salt and yoghurt and mix gently with the okra. Cover and cook for 10 minutes.

5 Add the curry leaves and cook a further 5 minutes. Serve with rice or poori (see breads).

LAU GHONTO / DRY DODDY

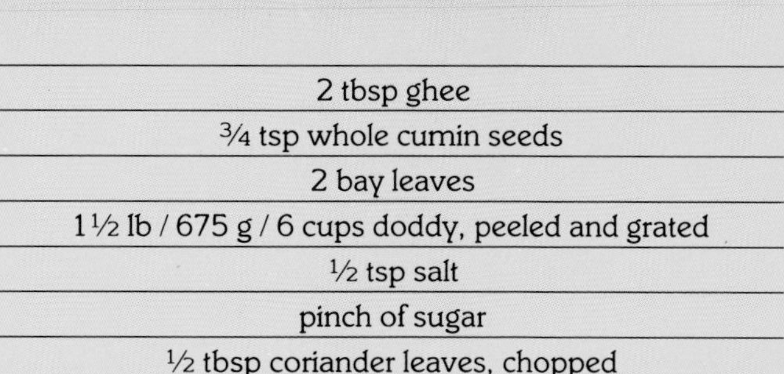

2 tbsp ghee

¾ tsp whole cumin seeds

2 bay leaves

1½ lb / 675 g / 6 cups doddy, peeled and grated

½ tsp salt

pinch of sugar

½ tbsp coriander leaves, chopped

1 Heat the ghee in a karai over medium heat and add the cumin seeds and bay leaves and let them sizzle for a few seconds. Add the doddy and fry for 3-4 minutes stirring constantly.

2 Cover, lower heat and cook for 20-25 minutes, stirring occasionally so that it does not stick to the bottom.

3 Remove the cover, turn the heat up to medium high, add the salt and sugar and, stirring constantly, fry till the doddy is browned and dry.

4 Serve sprinkled with the chopped coriander leaves.

SAAG PANIR / SPINACH WITH COTTAGE CHEESE

4 tbsp oil

6 oz / 175 g / 1 cup panir (see basic recipes), drained and cut into ½ inch or 1 cm cubes

1 large onion, finely sliced

4 cloves garlic, crushed

½ inch / 1 cm root ginger, grated

12 oz / 350 g / ⅔ cup frozen spinach, chopped

½ tsp ground turmeric

⅓ tsp chilli powder

1 tsp ground coriander

¾ tsp salt

1 Heat oil in a karai over medium high heat and fry the panir until brown. Set aside.

2 Add the onion, garlic, and ginger in the remaining oil and fry until golden.

3 Add the spinach, turmeric, chilli, coriander and salt and fry for 2-3 minutes.

4 Lower heat to medium, cover and cook a further 10 minutes.

5 Add the fried panir and, stirring constantly, cook until dry.

PANIR BHIYIA

2 tbsp oil
1 medium onion, finely chopped
1 clove garlic, crushed
10 oz / 275 g / 1⅔ cups panir (see basic recipes), drained
½ tsp ground turmeric
½ tsp salt
1 small green pepper, seeded and cut into ½ in / 1 cm pieces
1 large tomato, chopped
1-2 green chillis, chopped
1 tbsp coriander leaves, chopped

1 Heat the oil in a karai over medium heat and fry the onions and garlic for 5 minutes.

2 Add the panir, turmeric and salt and stir fry for 5 minutes.

3 Add the green pepper and tomato and cook for 8-10 minutes, stirring occasionally.

4 Sprinkle with the green chillis and coriander leaves and remove from the heat. Serve with poori (see breads).

MASALA KARELA / SPICY BITTER GOURD

- 2 large bitter gourds, finely sliced
- 1 tbsp oil
- 1 clove garlic, crushed
- 4-6 curry leaves
- 1-2 green chillis, chopped
- ½ tsp ground turmeric
- ¼ tsp chilli powder
- ½ tsp salt

1 Wash the slices of bitter gourd and pat dry.

Heat oil in a karai over medium high heat, add the garlic, curry leaves and green chillis and fry for 10 seconds.

3 Add the bitter gourd, turmeric, chilli and salt and fry for 10-15 minutes, stirring occasionally until tender.

MATER PANIR / COTTAGE CHEESE WITH PEAS

- 6 tbsp oil
- 10 oz / 275 g / 1⅔ cups panir (see basic recipes), drained and cut into ½ in / 1 cm pieces
- 6 tbsp onion mixture (see basic recipes)
- 1 tsp ground turmeric
- ½ tsp chilli powder
- 1 tsp ground coriander
- ¾ tsp salt
- 6 oz / 175 g / scant cup peas
- 8 fl oz / 225 ml / 1 cup water
- 1 tbsp coriander leaves, chopped (optional)

1 Heat the oil in a karai over medium high heat and fry the panir pieces until golden brown. Remove and drain on paper towels.

2 In the remaining oil add the onion mixture and fry for 3 minutes, stirring constantly. Add the turmeric, chilli, coriander and salt and continue to fry for a further 2-3 minutes.

3 Add the peas and mix thoroughl. Add the water and bring to the boil. Cover, lower heat to medium low and simmer for 5 minutes. Gently add the pieces of fried panir and simmer a further 10 minutes. Garnish with the coriander leaves and serve hot.

DHOKKAR DALNA / FRIED LENTIL CAKE CURRY

- 5oz / 125 g / ⅔ cup channa dal (see page 32), washed
- 30 fl oz / 825 ml / 3¾ cups water
- ¾ tsp salt
- ½ tsp ground turmeric
- ½ in / 1 cm root ginger, grated
- 2 tbsp desiccated coconut
- 2 green chillis
- 5 fl oz / 125 ml / ¾ cup water
- 14 tbsp oil
- 3 medium potatoes, cut into 1 in / 2.5 cm pieces
- ½ tsp whole cumin seeds
- 2 bay leaves
- 1 tsp ground turmeric
- ½ tsp chilli powder
- 1½ tsp ground cumin
- 1 tsp ground coriander
- ½ tsp salt
- 2 tomatoes, chopped
- 12 fl oz / 325 ml / 1½ cups water
- 1 tsp ghee (see basic recipes)
- ½ tsp garam masala (see basic recipes)

1 Soak the dal in 30 fl oz / 825 ml / 3¾ cups water overnight. Drain.

2 Mix the drained dal with ¾ tsp salt, ½ tsp turmeric, ginger, coconut, green chillies and 5 fl oz / 125 ml / ¾ cup water in a blender until you have a smooth creamy mixture.

3 In a karai, heat 8 tbsp of the oil over medium heat and fry the dal mixture until it leaves the side and a ball forms. Spread ½ in / 1 cm thick on a greased plate. Cool. Cut into 1 in / 2.5 cm squares.

4 Heat the rest of the oil in a karai over medium high heat and fry the dal squares a few at a time until golden brown. Set aside.

5 Fry the potatoes until lightly browned. Set aside.

6 Lower heat to medium, add the whole cumin seeds and bay leaves and let them sizzle for a few seconds.

7 Add the turmeric, chilli, coriander, salt and tomatoes and fry for 2 minutes. Add the water and bring to boil.

8 Add the potatoes, cover and cook for 10 minutes. Add the fried dal squares, cover again and cook until the potatoes are tender.

9 Add the ghee and sprinkle on the garam masala. Remove from the heat. Serve hot with rice or pillau.

SUKHI BEAN AUR NARIAL / BEANS WITH COCONUT

3 tbsp oil
½ tsp kalonji
2-3 dried red chillis
1 lb / 450 g green beans washed and cut into 1 in / 2.5 cm lengths
2 tbsp dessicated coconut
½ tsp salt

1 Heat oil in a karai over medium high heat, add the kalonji and chillis and let them sizzle for a few seconds.

2 Add the beans and stir fry for 10 minutes.

3 Add the coconut and salt and mix in thoroughly with the beans, and stirring constantly to avoid sticking cook a further 5-7 minutes. Serve with poori (see bread).

BAIGAN BHARTA / SPICY AUBERGINE (EGGPLANT)

1 lb / 450 g aubergines

3 tbsp oil

1 large onion, finely chopped

3 tomatoes, chopped

1 tbsp coriander leaves, chopped

1-2 green chillis, chopped

½ tsp ground turmeric

½ tsp chilli powder

¾ tsp ground coriander

¾ tsp salt

1 Place the aubergines under a pre-heated grill (broiler) for about 15 minutes, turning frequently until the skin turns black and the flesh soft. Peel off the skin and mash the flesh.

2 Heat the oil in a karai over medium heat and fry the onions until soft. Add the tomatoes, coriander leaves and green chillis and fry another 2-3 minutes.

3 Add the mashed aubergine, turmeric, chilli, coriander and salt and stir.

4 Fry for another 10-12 minutes and serve with chappatis (see bread).

MALAI BAIGAN / AUBERGINE (EGGPLANT) WITH SOUR CREAM

- 1 large aubergine, cut into ½ in / 1 cm slices
- ½ tsp salt
- ½ tsp ground turmeric
- pinch of sugar
- 8 tbsp oil
- pinch of asafetida
- 2 tbsp onion mixture (see basic recipes)
- 1 tsp ground cumin
- 1 tsp ground coriander
- ½ tsp chilli powder
- big pinch of sugar
- ½ tsp salt
- 5 fl oz / 125 g / ⅝ cup sour cream

1 Rub the aubergine slices with ½ tsp salt, ½ tsp turmeric and a pinch of sugar and set aside for 30 minutes.

2 Heat the oil in a large frying pan over medium high heat and fry the aubergine slices until brown. Drain on paper towels.

3 Lower heat to medium and add the asafetida to the remaining oil. Fry for 3-4 seconds and then add the onion mixture, cumin, coriander, chilli, sugar and salt and fry for 2 minutes.

4 Add the sour cream and mix with the spices. Add the fried aubergine slices. Cover and cook for 10 minutes. Serve with chappatis (see bread).

BAIGAN PORA / ROASTED AUBERGINE (EGGPLANT)

1 large aubergine
1 small onion, finely chopped
1-2 green chillis, finely chopped
½ tsp salt
2-3 tbsp mustard oil

1 Place the aubergine under a pre-heated grill (broiler) for about 15 minutes, turning frequently, until the skin becomes black and the flesh soft.

2 Peel the skin and mash the flesh.

3 Add the rest of the ingredients to the mashed aubergine and mix thoroughly.

SARSO BAIGAN / AUBERGINE (EGGPLANT) WITH MUSTARD

1 large aubergine, cut lengthwise
½ tsp salt
¼ tsp sugar
a big pinch of ground turmeric
8 tbsp oil
½ tsp kalonji
2 tsp ground mustard
½ tsp chilli powder
½ tsp ground turmeric
¾ tsp salt
1 tsp desiccated coconut
4 fl oz / 100 ml / ½ cup water

1 Rub the aubergine pieces with ½ tsp salt, sugar and a big pinch of ground turmeric and set aside for 30 minutes.

2 Heat the oil in a karai over medium heat and fry the aubergine pieces until brown. Drain on paper towels.

3 In the remaining oil add the kalonji and let it sizzle for a few seconds. Add the mustard, chilli, turmeric, salt and coconut. Fry for a minute and then add the water.

4 When the mixture starts to boil add the pieces of aubergine. Lower heat, cover and cook for 10 minutes.

JHINGE POSTO / ANGLED LOOFAH WITH POPPY SEEDS

2 tbsp poppy seeds
1-2 green chillis
4 tbsp oil
½ tsp kalonji
1-2 dried red chillis
2 lb / 900 g / approx 8 cups jhinge, peeled and sliced into ½ in / 1 cm pieces
½ tsp ground turmeric
¾ tsp salt

1 Grind the poppy seeds and green chillis to a paste.

2 Heat oil in a karai over medium high heat and add the kalonji and red chillis and let them sizzle for a few seconds.

3 Add the jhinge, turmeric and salt and stir for a few minutes.

4 Cover, lower heat to medium and cook for about 10-15 minutes. Add the paste.

5 Increase heat to medium high and, stirring constantly, fry until dry.

ALOO DAM / POTATO CURRY

6 tbsp oil
4 tbsp onion mixture (see basic recipes)
1½ lbs / 674 g / 6 cups small potatoes, peeled and boiled
½ tsp ground turmeric
½ tsp chilli powder
¾ tsp salt
big pinch of sugar
6 fl oz / 175 ml / ¾ cup water
½ tsp garam masala (see basic recipes)

1 Heat the oil in a karai over medium high heat and add the onion mixture and fry for 5 minutes, stirring frequently.

2 Add the potatoes, turmeric, chilli, salt and sugar and fry a further 2-3 minutes, stirring constantly so that it does not stick.

3 Add the water; when it starts to boil, cover, lower heat and simmer for about 10 minutes until you have a thick gravy.

4 Before removing from the heat sprinkle with the garam masala. Serve with paratha (see breads) or rice.

ALOO AUR CAPSICUM / POTATOES WITH GREENPEPPERS AND COCONUT

- 3 tbsp oil
- ½ tsp whole mustard seeds
- pinch of asafetida
- 6-8 curry leaves
- 1 lb / 450 g / 4 cups potatoes, boiled, peeled and diced into ½ in / 1 cm cubes
- 1 green pepper, seeded and cut into ½ in / 1 cm pieces
- 3 tbsp dessicated coconut
- ½ tsp salt
- 2 green chillis, chopped
- 1 tbsp coriander leaves, chopped

1 Heat the oil in a karai over medium heat, add the mustard seeds, asafetida and curry leaves and let them sizzle for 3-4 seconds.

2 Add the potatoes and green pepper and stir fry for 5 minutes.

3 Add the coconut and salt and, stirring occasionally, cook for another 5-7 minutes.

4 Before removing from the heat, sprinkle with the chillis and coriander leaves. Serve hot with poori (see bread).

ALOO GOBI DALNA / CAULIFLOWER AND POTATO CURRY

6 tbsp oil
1 lb / 450 g / 4 cups potatoes, peeled and quartered
1 small cauliflower, cut into large florets
pinch of asafetida
¾ tsp ground turmeric
½ tsp chilli powder
1½ tsp ground cumin
¾ tsp salt
big pinch of sugar
2 tomatoes, chopped
10 fl oz / 275 ml / 1¼ cups water
2 tsp ghee (see basic recipes)
½ tsp garam masala (see basic recipes)

1 Heat the oil in a karai over medium high heat.

2 Fry the potatoes a few pieces at a time until slightly brown. Remove and set aside.

3 Fry the cauliflower pieces a few at a time until brown spots appear on them. Remove and set aside.

4 Lower heat to medium, add the asafetida and after 3-4 seconds add the turmeric, chilli, cumin, salt and sugar. Mix the spices together, add the tomatoes and fry for 1 minute with the spices.

5 Add the water and bring to the boil. Put in the potatoes, cover and cook for 10 minutes.

6 Add the cauliflower, cover again and cook a further 5-7 minutes until the potatoes and cauliflower are tender.

7 Add the ghee and sprinkle with the garam masala. Remove from the heat and serve hot with rice and red lentils.

ALOO POSTO / POTATOES WITH POPPY SEEDS

3 tbsp oil
1 lb / 450 g / 4 cups potatoes, diced into ¾ in / 2 cm pieces
2 tbsp poppy seeds, ground
1 tbsp dessicated coconut
¾ tsp salt
a big pinch of sugar
2-3 green chillis, chopped

1 Heat oil in a karai over medium heat and fry the potatoes, stirring occasionally until nearly done, about 15 minutes.

2 Add the poppy seeds, coconut, salt, sugar and green chillis and continue cooking until the potatoes are tender. Serve with rice.

IMLEE ALOO / POTATOES WITH TAMARIND

6 tbsp oil
1 tsp whole cumin seeds
2 large onions, finely chopped
4 cloves garlic, crushed
1½ lbs / 775 g / 6 cups small potatoes, peeled and boiled
½ in / 1 cm root ginger, grated
½ tsp ground turmeric
¼ tsp chilli powder
¾ tsp salt
1 tsp sugar
3 fl oz / 75 ml / ⅜ cup thick tamarind juice (see basic recipes)
½ tsp roasted ground cumin (see basic recipes)

1 Heat oil in a karai over medium high heat, add the cumin seeds and let them sizzle for a few seconds.

2 Add the onions and garlic and fry them until the onions are soft.

3 Lower the heat to medium low, add the potatoes and ginger and fry for 5-7 minutes, stirring occasionally.

4 Add the turmeric, chilli, salt, sugar and tamarind juice and cook for 10-15 minutes.

5 Before removing from the heat, sprinkle with the roasted ground cumin.

ALOO CHOKKA / DRY POTATOES

6 tbsp mustard oil

¾ tsp kalonji

1½ lb / 675 g potatoes, cut into thin strips

½ tsp ground turmeric

1 tsp salt

3-4 green chillis

1 Heat oil in a karai over medium high heat. Add the kalonji and let it sizzle for a few seconds.

2 Add the potatoes and fry for 2-3 minutes.

3 Add the turmeric, salt and chillis and mix in with the potatoes.

4 Cover, lower heat to medium low and, stirring occasionally, cook for another 15-20 minutes until the potatoes are tender.

BAKED GOBI / ROASTED CAULIFLOWER

4 medium tomatoes
1 large onion
3 cloves garlic
½ in / 1 cm root ginger
2 tbsp ghee (see basic recipes)
¾ tsp ground turmeric
½ tsp chilli powder
½ tsp garam masala (see basic recipes)
6 oz / 175 g / scant cup peas
½ tsp salt
1 medium-sized cauliflower, blanched

1 Blend the tomatoes, onion, garlic and ginger in a blender until you have a paste.

2. Heat the ghee in a frying pan over medium heat and add the paste, turmeric, chilli and garam masala and stir fry until the ghee and spices separate, about 5-6 minutes.

3 Add the peas and salt and cook a further 5 minutes, stirring constantly. Remove from the heat.

4 Place the cauliflower in a large oven-proof dish and pour the spices over it. Place in a preheated oven 375°F / 190°C / Gas Mark 5 for 30-35 minutes. Serve on a flat plate with the peas and spices poured over.

ALOO GOBI AUR MATER / CAULIFLOWER WITH POTATOES AND PEAS

- 4 tbsp oil
- 2 medium onions, finely chopped
- 1 lb / 450 g / 4 cups potatoes, diced into ¾ in / 2 cm pieces
- 1 small cauliflower, cut into ¾ in / 2 cm pieces
- ½ tsp ground turmeric
- ⅓ tsp chilli powder
- 1 tsp ground cumin
- 2 tomatoes, chopped
- 1 tsp salt
- ¼ tsp sugar
- 7 oz / 200 g / 1 cup peas
- ½ tsp garam masala (see basic recipes)

1 Heat the oil in a karai over medium high heat.

2 Add the onions and fry for 3-4 minutes until light brown.

3 Add the potatoes and cauliflower and stir. Add the turmeric, chilli, cumin, tomatoes, salt and sugar. Stir and fry for 2-3 minutes.

4 Add the peas, cover and lower heat to medium low and cook for about 20 minutes until the potatoes and cauliflower are tender. During the cooking period stir the vegetables a few times to stop them sticking.

5 Sprinkle with garam masala before serving.

ALOO GOBI CHOKKA / DRY POTATO AND CAULIFLOWER

3 tbsp oil
¾ tsp kalonji
3-4 green chillis, split in half
1 small cauliflower, cut into ¾ in / 2 cm pieces
1 lb / 455 g / 4 cups potatoes, diced into ¾ in / 2 cm pieces
¾ tsp salt

1 Heat oil in a karai over medium high heat and add the kalonji and green chillis. Let them sizzle for a few seconds.

2 Add the cauliflower and potatoes and stir for 1-2 minutes.

3 Lower heat to medium low, cover and cook for 15-20 minutes, stirring occasionally to stop it sticking to the bottom of the karai.

4 Add the salt, turn up the heat and, stirring constantly, fry until the potatoes and cauliflower are tender. Serve with lucchis (see bread).

VEGETABLES

KHUMBI, ALOO AUR PYAZ / MUSHROOM WITH POTATOES AND ONIONS

5 tbsp oil
1 large potato, diced into ¾ in / 2 cm pieces
4 cardamoms
1½ in / 4 cm stick cinnamon
2 bay leaves
1 large onion, finely sliced
2 cloves garlic, crushed
¾ in / 2 cm ginger, grated
1 tsp ground turmeric
½ tsp chilli powder
½ tsp salt
a big pinch sugar
1½ tsp white vinegar
8 oz / 225 g / 4 cups mushrooms, quartered

1 Heat oil in a karai over medium high heat. Add the potatoes and fry for 2-3 minutes until light golden in colour. Remove the potatoes and set aside.

2 To the same oil add the cardamoms, cinnamon and bay leaves and let them sizzle for a few seconds.

3 Add the onions, garlic and ginger and fry for 4-5 minutes until soft and golden.

4 Add the turmeric, chilli, salt, sugar and vinegar and fry, stirring continuously, for another minute.

5 Add the mushrooms and potatoes to the spice mixture and mix thoroughly.

6 Lower heat to medium, cover and cook for about 15 minutes until the potatoes are tender.

AVIAL / VEGETABLES IN A YOGHURT AND COCONUT SAUCE

- 2 green bananas, peeled and cut into ½ in / 1 cm pieces
- 4 oz / 100 g / 1 cup green beans, cut into ½ in / 1 cm pieces
- 2 oz / 50 g / ½ cup carrots, diced into ¼ in / .5 cm cubes
- 2 oz / 50 g / ¼ cup peas
- 12 fl oz / 325 ml / 1½ cups water
- ¾ tsp chilli powder
- ½ tsp ground turmeric
- ¾ tsp salt
- 8 fl oz / 225 ml / 1 cup unsweetened yoghurt
- 2 green chillis, chopped
- 1 tsp ground coriander
- 2 tbsp desiccated coconut
- 1 tbsp oil
- ½ tsp whole mustard seeds
- 6-8 curry leaves

1 Place the vegetables, chilli powder, turmeric, salt and water in a large saucepan and bring to boil. Simmer for about 20 minutes till the vegetables are tender. Remove from the heat.

2 Whisk the yoghurt, green chillis, coriander and coconut together and set aside.

3 In a large saucepan heat the oil over medium high heat. Add the mustard seeds and curry leaves, and after 5-6 seconds add the vegetables with the liquid. Cook for 2-3 minutes. Lower the heat and add the yoghurt mixture and, stirring occasionally, cook for a further 4-5 minutes. Serve with rice.

MASALA KADDU / PUMPKIN WITH SPICES

2 tbsp oil

½ tsp kalonji

2 dried red chillis

1 large onion, finely sliced

1 lb / 450 g / 4 cups pumpkin, diced into ½ in / 1 cm cubes

½ tsp ground turmeric

½ tsp chilli powder

½ tsp salt

1 Heat oil in a karai over medium high heat, add the kalonji and red chillis and let them sizzle for about 15 seconds. Add the onions and fry until golden.

2 Add the pumpkin, turmeric, chilli and salt and stir fry for 2-3 minutes. Cover, lower heat to medium and cook a further 10 minutes. Serve hot with lucchi (see bread).

KARHI / YOGHURT CURRY

Pakoras
4 tbsp gram flour (chick pea flour)
¼ tsp salt
pinch of ground turmeric
about 1½ oz / 40 g / ¼ cup water
oil for deep frying
Curry
8 fl oz / 225 ml / 1 cup unsweetened yoghurt
12 fl oz / 325 ml / 1½ cups water
1 tbsp gram flour
1 tbsp oil
¼ tsp fenugreek seeds
pinch of asafetida
6-8 curry leaves
2 green chillis, chopped
½ tsp ground turmeric
½ tsp chilli powder
½ tsp salt

Pakoras

1 Mix the gram flour, salt and turmeric. Add enough water to make a thick batter.

2 Heat the oil over medium high heat. Drop a tablespoon of the batter at a time into the hot oil and fry till crisp and golden. Drain and set aside.

3 Whisk the yoghurt, water and gram flour till smooth.

4 Place the fried pakoras in a bowl of water for 3-4 minutes. Gently squeeze out as much water as possible and set aside.

5 Heat 1 tablespoon of oil in a large saucepan over medium heat, add the fenugreek, asafetida, curry leaves and green chillis and let them sizzle for 10 seconds.

6 Add the yoghurt mixture, tumeric, chilli and salt and slowly bring to the boil.

7 Lower the heat, add the pakoras and simmer for about 10 minutes till the sauce has thickened. Serve hot with rice.

The 'King of Rice' is the Basmati variety that comes from Dehra Dun – one of the hill stations founded by the British as a summer retreat. This rice carries a unique flavour when cooked and is by far the best quality. Other types of rice are Pakistani Basmati rice, Patna rice and Tilds rice. American long-grain rice is also adequate for the preparation of Indian meals.

MATER PILLAU / PEA PILLAU

3 tbsp oil
½ tsp whole cumin seeds
1 medium onion, finely chopped
4 oz / 100 g / ½ cup peas
12 oz / 325 g / 1½ cups basmati rice, washed and drained
1 tsp salt
30 fl oz / 825 ml / 3¾ cups water

1 Heat oil in a large saucepan over medium heat, add the cumin seeds and let them sizzle for a few seconds.

2 Add the onion and fry until soft. Add the peas, rice and salt and stir fry for about 5 minutes. Add the water and bring to boil.

3 Cover tightly, lower heat to very low and cook for about 20 minutes until all the water has been absorbed. Fluff the pillau with a fork and serve hot.

KHUMBI PILLAU / MUSHROOM PILLAU

2 tbsp oil
2 bay leaves
2 in / 5 cm cinnamon stick
4 cardamoms
1 large onion, finely chopped
6 oz / 175 g / 3 cups mushrooms, sliced
12 oz / 325 g / 1½ cups basmati rice, washed and drained
1 tsp salt
30 fl oz / 825 ml / 3¾ cups water

1 Heat oil in a large saucepan over medium high heat. Add the bay leaves, cinnamon and cardamoms and let them sizzle for a few seconds.

2 Add the onion and fry until soft. Add the mushrooms and fry for about 5 minutes until all the moisture has been absorbed.

3. Add the rice and salt and stir fry for 2-3 minutes. Add the water and bring to the boil.

4 Cover tightly, lower heat to very low and cook for about 20 minutes until all the water has been absorbed. Fluff the pillau with a fork and serve hot.

SADA CHAWAL 1 / PLAIN RICE 1

12 oz / 325 g / 1½ cups basmati rice

30 fl oz / 825 ml / 3¾ cups cold water

1 Rinse the rice three or four times in cold water. Drain.

2 Place the drained rice in a large saucepan and pour in the measured amount of water. Bring it to the boil rapidly over a high heat. Stir.

3 Lower heat to very low, cover and cook for about 20 minutes until all the water has evaporated.

4 Fluff the rice with a fork and serve hot.

SADA CHAWAL 2 / PLAIN RICE 2

12 oz / 325 g / 1½ cups basmati rice

5 pints / 2.75 litre / 12½ cups water

1 Rinse the rice in cold water three or four times. Soak the rice in 3 pints / 1.6 litre / 7½ cups of water for 1 hour. Drain.

2 Place the drained rice in a large saucepan, add the 5 pints / 2.75 litre / 12½ cups water. Bring it to the boil over high heat and boil rapidly for 5 minutes until the rice is cooked. Drain the rice, fluff it with a fork and serve hot.

GHEE BHAT / FRIED RICE

12 oz / 325 g / 1½ cups basmati rice, cooked and cooled
3 tbsp ghee (see basic recipes)
2 bay leaves
2 in / 5 cm cinnamon stick
4 cardamoms
3 large onions, finely sliced
3 green chillis, cut lengthwise
1 tsp salt
½ tsp sugar
2 tbsp raisins (optional)

1 Heat the ghee in a large frying pan over medium high heat. Add the bay leaves, cinnamon, cardamoms and let them sizzle for a few seconds.

2 Add the onions and chillis and fry until the onions are golden brown.

3 Add the rice, salt, sugar and raisins and continue frying until the rice is thoroughly heated up.

NARIYAL AUR DUDH PILLAU / PILLAU WITH COCONUT AND MILK

12 oz / 325 g / 1½ cups basmati rice, rinsed and drained
2 tbsp dessicated coconut
2-3 green chillis
1 tsp salt
½ tsp sugar
2 tbsp raisins
1 tbsp pistachio nuts, skinned and cut into thin strips
2 bay leaves
2 in / 5 cm cinnamon stick
4 cardamoms
3 tbsp ghee (see basic recipes)
1 pint / 550 ml / 2½ cups milk
10 fl oz / 275 ml / 1¼ cups water

1 Mix the rice with the coconut, chillis, salt, sugar, raisins, pistachios, bay leaves, cinnamon and cardamoms.

2 Heat the ghee in a large saucepan over medium heat. Add the rice mixture and sauté for 5 minutes, stirring constantly.

3 Add the milk and water, increase the heat to high and bring it to the boil. Stir.

4 Lower heat to very low, cover and cook for about 20 minutes until all the liquid has evaporated. Fluff the pillau with a fork and serve hot.

KHICHURI 1 / RICE AND LENTIL CURRY

8 oz / 225 g / 1 cup basmati rice, washed and drained
2 oz / 50 g / ¼ cup moong dal washed and drained
25 fl oz / 700 ml / 3 cups water
1½ tbsp ghee (see basic recipes)

1 Mix the rice and dal and soak in plenty of water for 1 hour. Drain.

2 Add the rice and dal mixture to the measured water in a large saucepan and bring to the boil over a high heat. Turn heat down to very low, cover and cook for about 20 minutes until all the water has been absorbed. Remove from heat.

3 In a small pan heat the ghee until very hot and pour it over the cooked rice and dal. Mix. Serve hot with Sai bhaji, yoghurt and poppadum.

KHICHURI 2 / RICE WITH LENTILS

3 oz / 75 g / ⅓ cup moong dal
3 oz / 75 g / ⅓ cup red lentils, washed
6 tbsp oil
2 bay leaves
2 in / 5 cm cinnamon stick
4 cardamoms
3 cloves garlic, crushed
1 in / 2.5 cm root ginger, grated
1 large onion, finely sliced
1 tsp ground turmeric
½ tsp chilli powder
1 tsp salt
⅓ tsp sugar
1 tomato, chopped
3 oz / 75 g / ⅓ cup basmati rice, washed and drained
2¼ pints / 1.25 litre / 5½ cups water
3-4 green chillis, halved lengthwise

1 In a small pan dry roast the moong dal over medium heat, until it turns light brown. Remove from the heat, wash thoroughly, and mix with the red lentils. Put in a sieve to drain.

2 Heat oil in a large saucepan over medium heat. Add the bay leaves, cinnamon stick and cardamoms and let them sizzle for a few seconds.

3 Add garlic, ginger and onion and fry until onion is golden brown.

4 Add the turmeric, chilli, salt, sugar and tomato and mix thoroughly. Add the rice and the lentils and continue to fry for 5-7 minutes.

5 Add the water, and when it starts to boil, lower heat and simmer for about 35-40 minutes.

6 Just before removing from the heat, add the chillis. Serve with melted ghee (see basic recipe) and pakoras (see bread).

Breads can be fried or grilled. An ordinary gas or electric oven can be used to grill the various breads, but for best results a Tandoor should be used. This is a barrel-shaped clay oven which gives breads that special charcoal flavour. Try grilling breads on a barbecue and see how your friends react.

Indians eat these breads with their fingers. Tear a piece of bread and dip it into a plate of curry or wrap a small piece of bread around a dry vegetable. And don't forget to lick your fingers!

POORI / DEEP FRIED BROWN BREAD

8 oz / 225 g / 2¼ cups wholewheat flour
½ tsp salt
2 tbsp oil
about 3½ fl oz / 90 ml / scant ½ cup hot water
oil for deep frying

1 Sieve together with flour and salt. Rub in the oil. Add enough water to make a stiff dough.

2 Put the dough on a floured surface and knead for about 10 minutes till soft and smooth.

3 Divide the mixture into 20 balls.

4 Take one ball at a time, flatten it on a slightly oiled surface and roll into rounds of 4 in / 10 cm across. (Do not stack the rolled pooris on one another as they might stick together).

5 Heat oil in a karai until very hot, add a poori, pressing the middle with a slotted spoon so that it puffs up. Quickly turn and cook the other side for a few seconds. Drain and serve hot.

ALOO PARATHA / STUFFED LAYERED BREAD

Filling:
1 lb / 450 g / 5 cups potatoes, boiled and mashed
1 small onion, finely chopped
1-2 green chillis, finely chopped
1 tbsp coriander leaves, chopped
¾ tsp salt
¾ tsp ground roasted cumin (see basic recipes)
Dough:
12 oz / 325 g / 2¾ cups plain flour
½ tsp salt
4 tbsp oil
about 6 fl oz / 175 ml / ¾ cup hot water
ghee (see basic recipes) for frying

Filling:

1 Mix all the ingredients together and set aside.

Dough:

1 Sieve the flour and salt together. Rub in the oil. Add enough water to form a stiff dough. Knead for about 10 minutes until you have a soft smooth dough. Divide into 20 balls.

2 Roll out two balls into 4 in / 10 cm rounds each. Place about 1½-2 tbsp of the filling on one of the rounds and spread it evenly. Place the other round over the filling, sealing the edges with a little water.

3 Roll out gently into 7 in / 18 cm rounds, and be careful that no filling comes out. Roll out all the parathas in a similar manner.

4 Heat a frying pan over medium heat. Place a paratha in the frying pan and cook for about 1 minute until brown spots appear. Turn and cook the other side.

5 Add two tsp of ghee and cook for 2-3 minutes until golden brown. Turn and cook the other side, adding more ghee if required. Make all the parathas in the same way. Serve warm.

BATORA / YOGHURT BREAD

8 oz / 225 g / 2¼ cups plain flour
1½ tsp baking powder
½ tsp salt
1 tsp sugar
1 egg, beaten
about 3 tbsp yoghurt
oil for deep frying

1 Sieve the flour, baking powder and salt together. Mix in the sugar.

2 Add the beaten egg and enough yoghurt to form a stiff dough. Knead for 10-15 minutes until you have a soft, smooth dough. Cover with a cloth and let it rest for 3-4 hours.

3 Knead again on a floured surface for 5 minutes. Divide into 12-14 balls.

4 Roll out on a floured surface into 5 in / 12.5 cm rounds.

5 Heat the oil in a karai over high heat. Fry the batora, pressing in the middle with a slotted spoon so that it puffs up. Turn and cook the other side for a few seconds until lightly browned. Drain. Serve hot with Kabli channa/chole (see pages 40/41).

MATER KACHORI / STUFFED DEEP FRIED BREAD

Filling:
1 tbsp ghee (see basic recipes)
pinch of asafetida
¼ in / 0.5 cm root ginger, grated
8 oz / 225 g / 1-1½ cups peas, boiled and mashed
¼ tsp chilli powder
¼ tsp salt
½ tsp garam masala (see basic recipes)
Dough:
8 oz / 225 g / 2¼ cups plain flour
½ tsp salt
1½ tsp ghee (see basic recipes)
approx. 4 fl oz / 100 ml / ½ cup hot water
oil for deep frying

Filling:

1 Heat the ghee in a karai over medium heat, add the asafetida and ginger and fry for a few seconds.

2 Add the mashed peas, chilli and salt and, stirring constantly, fry for about 5 minutes until the mixture leaves the sides and forms a ball. Mix in the garam masala and set aside to cool.

Dough:

1 Sieve the flour and salt together. Rub in the ghee. Add enough water to make a stiff dough. Knead for about 10 minutes to form a soft pliable dough. Divide into 20 balls.

2 Insert your thumb into the middle of each ball to form a cup. Fill with 1 teaspoon of the filling. Seal the top and make it into a ball again.

3 Flatten and roll into 4 in / 10 cm rounds on a slightly oiled surface (take care that no holes appear when rolling).

4 Heat oil in a karai until very hot. Gently put in a kachori, press the middle so that it puffs up. Turn and fry the other side until lightly golden. Drain on paper towels and serve hot with aloo dam (see page 66).

LUCCHI / DEEP FRIED WHITE BREAD

12 oz / 350 g / 2¾ cups plain flour
½ tsp salt
2 tbsp oil
about 6 fl oz / 175 ml / ¾ cup hot water
oil for deep frying

1 Sieve the flour and salt together. Rub in the oil.

2 Slowly add enough water to form a stiff dough. Knead for about 10 minutes until you have a soft pliable dough.

3 Divide the dough into about 40 small balls and flatten each ball.

4 Roll out a few balls on a slightly oily surface into rounds of 4 in / 10 cm across (do not roll out all the balls at the same time as they tend to stick).

5 Heat oil in a karai over high heat. Put in a lucchi and press the middle with a slotted spoon as this causes the lucchi to puff up. Turn and cook the other side for a few seconds. Drain and serve hot.

NAAN / LEAVEN BREAD

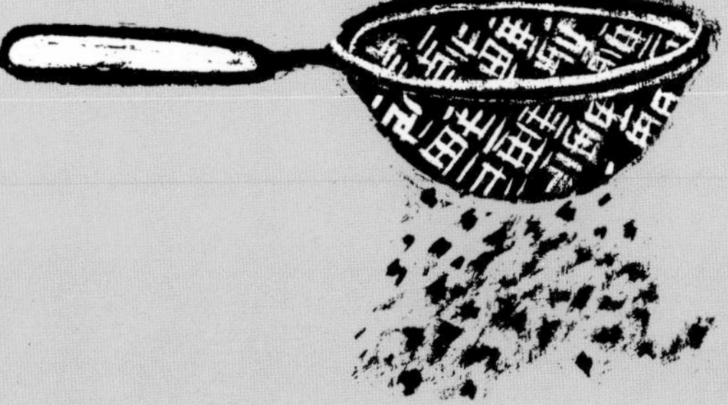

- 1 tsp dried yeast
- 1 tsp sugar
- 3 fl oz / 75 ml / 3⁄8 cup lukewarm water
- 10 oz / 275 g / 2¾ cups plain flour
- ½ tsp salt
- ¾ tsp baking powder
- 1 tbsp oil
- about 3 tbsp plain yoghurt

1 Stir the yeast and sugar into the water and set aside for 15-20 minutes until the liquid is frothy.

2 Sieve together the flour, salt and baking powder. Make a well in the middle, add the yeast liquid, oil and yoghurt and knead for about 10 minutes till soft and no longer sticky.

3 Place the dough in an oiled plastic bag and set aside in a warm place for 2-3 hours until double in size.

4 Knead again for 1-2 minutes and divide into 12 balls. Roll into 7 in / 18 cm rounds.

5 Place as many as possible on a baking sheet and put in a preheated oven 400°F / 200°C / Gas Mark 6 for 4-5 minutes each side until brown spots appear. Place them for a few seconds under a hot grill (broiler) until slightly browned.

6 Wrap the cooked ones in foil while cooking the others.

CHAPPATI / WHOLEWHEAT UNLEAVEN BREAD

10 oz / 275 g / 2¾ cups wholewheat flour
½ tsp salt
about 6 fl oz / 175 ml / ¾ cup hot water
2 tbsp melted ghee (see basic recipes)

1 Sieve the flour and salt together. Add enough water to form a soft dough.

2 Knead for about 10 minutes until no longer sticky. Cover and set aside for 1 hour.

3 Divide the dough into 12-14 balls. On a floured surface roll each ball into 6 in / 15 cm rounds.

4 Preheat the grill to very hot.

5 Heat a frying pan over medium heat and place a chappati on it. Cook the chappati for 2 minutes until brown spots appear. Turn and cook the other side in the same way.

6 Take the chappati and place it under the hot grill for a few seconds; it will puff up. Turn and cook the other side for a few seconds until it also puffs up.

7 Place the chappati in a dish and brush with a little melted ghee. Cover and keep warm while cooking the others.

PARATHA / LAYERED BREAD

12 oz / 350 g / 2¾ cups plain flour

½ tsp salt

4 tbsp oil

about 6 fl oz / 175 ml / ¾ cup hot water

3 heaped tbsp ghee, melted (see basic recipe)

1 Sieve the flour and salt together. Rub in the oil.

2 Slowly add the water to form a soft dough. Knead for about 10 minutes until it is no longer sticky.

3 Divide the dough into 16 balls. Flatten a ball on a lightly floured surface and roll into an 8 in / 20 cm circle.

4 Brush a little ghee on this and fold in half, brush on a little more ghee and fold into a small triangle. Roll out the triangle quite thinly on the floured surface.

5 Heat a frying pan over medium heat and place a rolled triangle on it. Heat each side for 1 minute until brown specks appear. Keep aside. Cook each triangle in this manner.

6 Add the ghee and gently fry the parathas one at a time for 1-2 minutes, turning once, until golden brown. (While cooking the parathas, keep the fried parathas warm by wrapping in foil).

Indians look forward to their dessert and it is often the climax of the meal. Most sweets are milk-based and can be prepared in advance.

SANDESH / CHEESE FUDGE

12 oz / 350 g / 2 cups panir (see page 00), drained

3 oz / 75 g / ⅓ cup sugar

1 tbsp pistachio nuts, finely chopped

1 Place the panir in a plate and rub with the palm of your hand till smooth and creamy.

2 Put the panir in a karai over medium heat, add the sugar and, stirring constantly, cook till it leaves the sides and a ball forms.

3 Remove from the heat and spread on a plate ½ in / 1 cm thick. Cool slightly, sprinkle with the nuts and cut into small diamonds. Serve warm or cold.

SOOJI HALVA / SEMOLINA HALVA

3 tbsp ghee (see basic recipes)
1 oz / 25 g / 1/4 cup almonds, blanched and sliced
4 oz / 100 g / 2/3 cup semolina
1 tbsp raisins
14 fl ozs / 400 ml / 1 3/4 cups milk
2 1/2 ozs / 60 g / 1/4 cup sugar

1 Heat ghee in a karai over medium heat.

2 Add the almonds and fry for 1-2 minutes until golden brown. Remove with a slotted spoon and drain on a paper towel.

3 Put in the semolina and fry, stirring continuously, until golden. Add the raisins and mix with the semolina.

4 Add milk and sugar and continue stirring until the mixture leaves the sides of the karai and a ball forms.

5 Serve on a flat dish garnished with the almonds.

MALPOA / FRITTERS IN SYRUP

7 oz / 200 g / 1¾ cups plain flour
1½ tsp baking powder
6 fl oz / 175 ml / ¾ cup yoghurt
approx 6 fl oz / 175 ml / ¾ cup milk
8 oz / 225 g / 1 cup sugar
16 fl oz / 450 ml / 2 cups water
oil for deep frying

1 Sieve together the flour and baking powder. Mix in the yoghurt. Add enough milk to make a thick batter.

2 Boil the sugar and water together for 10 minutes.

3 Heat the oil in a karai over medium high heat. Drop in 1 tablespoon of the batter at a time and fry until crisp and brown. Drain on paper towels.

4 Soak the fried malpoa in the syrup for 5 minutes. Serve in a little syrup, hot or cold.

PAYODHI / BAKED YOGHURT

14.5 oz / 410 g / 1¾ cups evaporated milk
14 oz / 397 g / 1¾ cups condensed milk
18 oz / 500 g / 2¼ cups yoghurt
1 tbsp pistachio nuts, skinned and chopped

1 Preheat oven to 450°F / 225°C / Gas Mark 5.

2 Whisk the evaporated milk, condensed milk and yoghurt together for 1 minute.

3 Pour into an oven-proof dish and place in the preheated oven.

4 Turn the oven off after 6 minutes and leave the dish in the oven overnight.

5 Chill. Serve garnished with the chopped pistachio nuts.

SHRIKHAND / YOGHURT WITH SAFFRON

20 fl oz / 550 ml / 2½ cups yoghurt
¼ tsp saffron
1 tbsp warm milk
4 oz / 100 g / ½ cup castor sugar
2 tbsp pistachio nuts, skinned and chopped

1 Put the yoghurt in a muslin bag and hang it up for 4-5 hours to get rid of the excess water.

2 Soak the saffron in the milk for 30 minutes.

3 Whisk together the drained yoghurt, sugar and saffron milk till smooth and creamy.

4 Put in a dish and garnish with the nuts. Chill until set.

(Any seasonal fruit may be added while whisking).

RASSOGOLLA / CHEESE BALLS IN SYRUP

11 oz / 300 g / 1⅓ cups panir (see basic recipes), drained

6 oz / 175 g / 1 cup ricotta cheese

12 oz / 350 g / 1½ cups sugar

48 fl oz / 1.35 litre / 6 cups water

1 Rub the panir and ricotta cheese with the palm of your hand until smooth and creamy. Divide into 16 balls.

2 Boil the sugar and water for 5 minutes over medium heat. Put the balls in the syrup and boil for 40 minutes.

3 Cover and continue to boil for another 30 minutes. Serve warm or cold.

KAMLA KHIR / KHIR WITH ORANGES

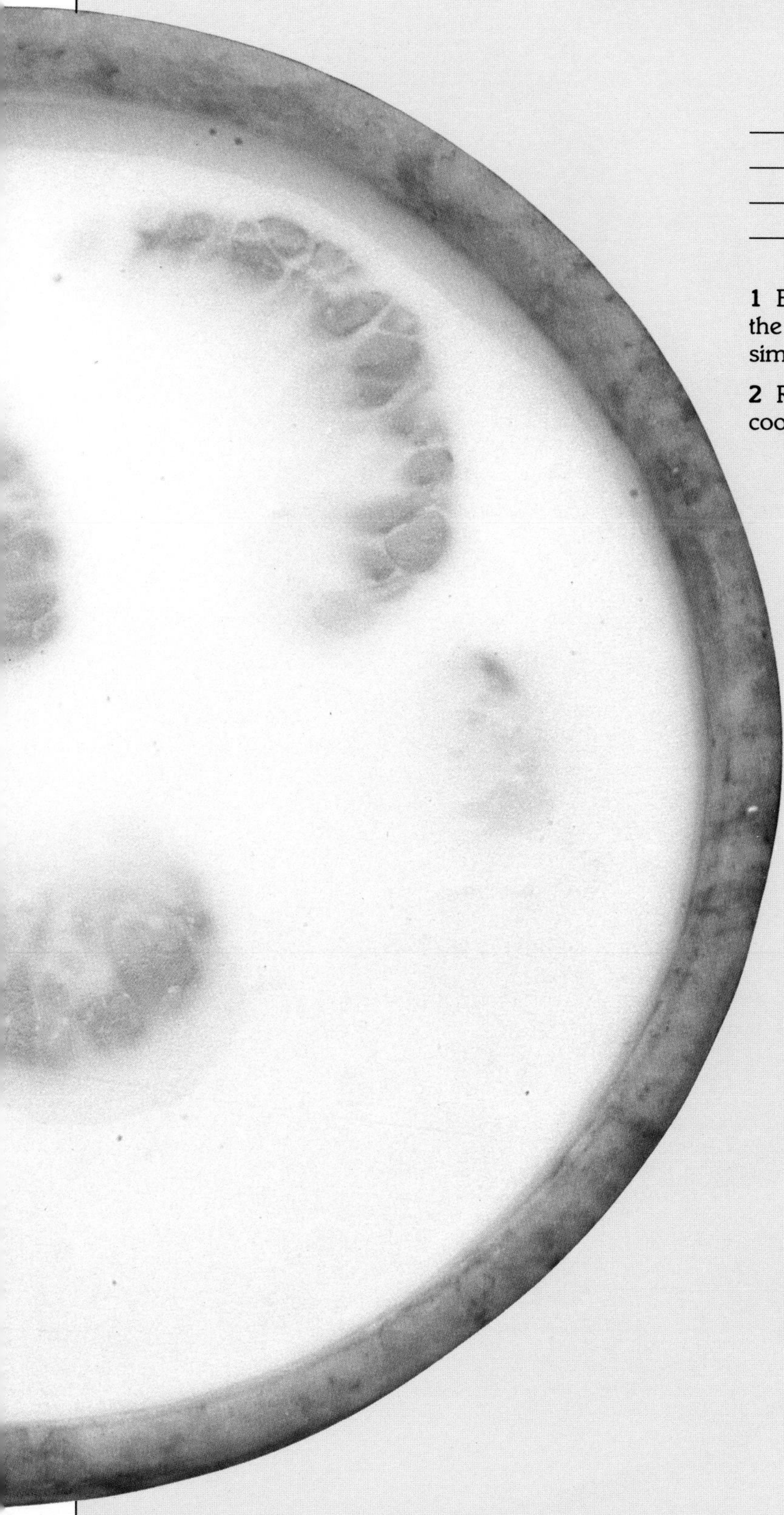

2 pints / 1.15 litres / 5 cups milk
1½ oz / 40 g / scant ¼ cup sugar
2 oranges, peeled

1 Boil the milk in a large saucepan, stirring constantly. Add the sugar and stir. Reduce heat and, stirring occasionally, simmer until it is reduced to ¾ pint / 425 ml / 1⅞ cups. Cool.

2 Remove all the pith from the oranges and slice. Add to the cooled milk. Serve chilled.

GAJAR HALVA / CARROT HALVA

1 lb / 450 g / 4 cups carrots, peeled and grated
1½ pints / 850 ml / 3¾ cups milk
5 oz / 125 g / ⅔ cups sugar
3 cardamoms
4 tbsp ghee (see basic recipes)
2 tbsp raisins
2 tbsp pistachio nuts, skinned and chopped

1 Place the carrots, milk, sugar and cardamoms in a large saucepan and bring to the boil. Lower heat to medium low and, stirring occasionally, cook until all the liquid has evaporated.

2 Heat the ghee in a large frying pan over medium heat, add the cooked carrots, raisins and pistachios and, stirring constantly, fry for 15-20 minutes until it is dry and turned reddish in colour. Serve hot or cold.

CHALER PAYESH / RICE PUDDING

2 pints / 1.2 litres / 5 cups milk
1 tbsp basmati rice, washed
2 tbsp sugar
1 tbsp raisins
½ tsp ground cardamoms
1½ tbsp pistachio nuts, skinned and chopped

1 Bring the milk to the boil in a large pan, stirring continuously.

2 Lower the heat and simmer for 20 minutes. Add the rice and sugar and continue simmering for another 35-40 minutes until the milk has thickened and reduced to 1 pint / 1.1 litres / 2½ cups. During the cooking time stir occasionally to stopp the milk sticking to the bottom of the pan.

3 Add the raisins and cardamoms and, stirring constantly, cook for a further 3-4 minutes.

4 Remove from the heat and garnish with the nuts. Serve hot or cold.

CHUTNEYS
AND RELISHES

BOONDI RAITA / YOGHURT WITH BOONDI

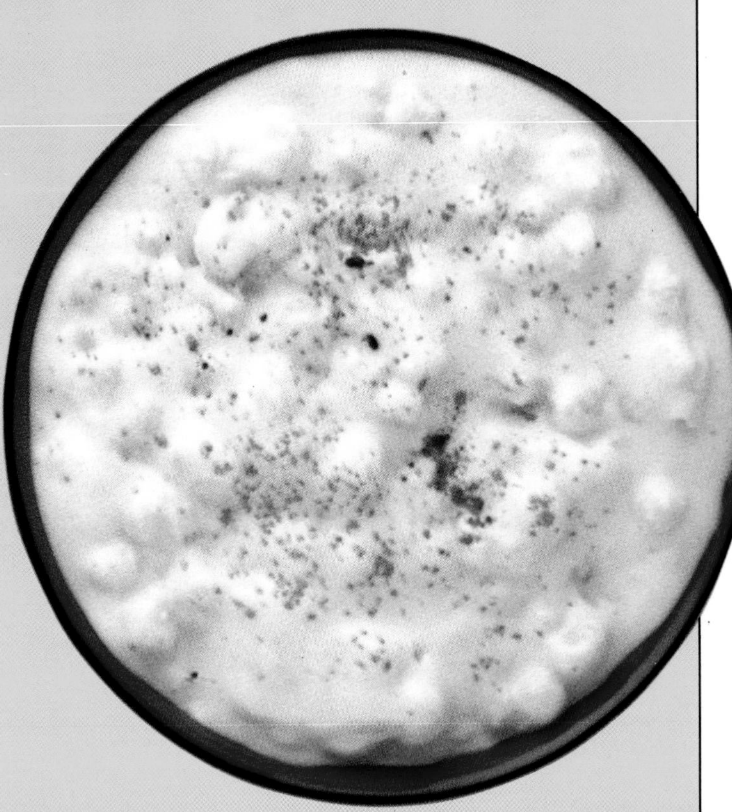

3 oz / 75 g / 1 cup boondi
12 fl oz / 325 g / 1½ cups unsweetened yoghurt
½ tsp salt
½ tsp chilli powder
pinch of paprika
pinch of garam masala (see basic recipes)

1 Soak the boondi in a little cold water for 10-15 minutes.

2 Beat the yoghurt in a bowl until smooth. Add the salt and chilli powder and stir.

3 Gently squeeze the boondi to remove the water and add to the spiced yoghurt. Mix well and chill. Before serving sprinkle with paprika and garam masala.

KHEERA RAITA / YOGHURT WITH CUCUMBER

12 fl oz / 325 ml / 1½ cups unsweetened yoghurt
1-2 green chillis, chopped
2 tbsp coriander leaves, chopped
½ cucumber, finely sliced
½ tsp chilli powder
½ tsp ground roasted cumin (see basic recipes)
½ tsp salt

1 In a bowl whisk the yoghurt until smooth.

2 Add all the other ingredients and stir in well. Chill.

ALOO RAITA / YOGHURT WITH POTATOES

- 16 fl oz / 450 ml / 2 cups unsweetened yoghurt
- 10 oz / 275 g / 2½ cups potatoes, boiled and diced into ¼ in / 0.5 cm cubes
- 1 small onion, finely chopped
- ½ tsp salt
- ¼ tsp ground black pepper
- ½ tsp ground roasted cumin
- 1 green chilli, chopped
- 1 tbsp coriander leaves

1 Beat the yoghurt in a bowl until smooth.

2 Add the potatoes, onions, salt, pepper and cumin and gently mix. Chill.

3 Serve sprinkled with the chilli and coriander leaves.

BAIGAN RAITA / YOGHURT WITH AUBERGINE (EGGPLANT)

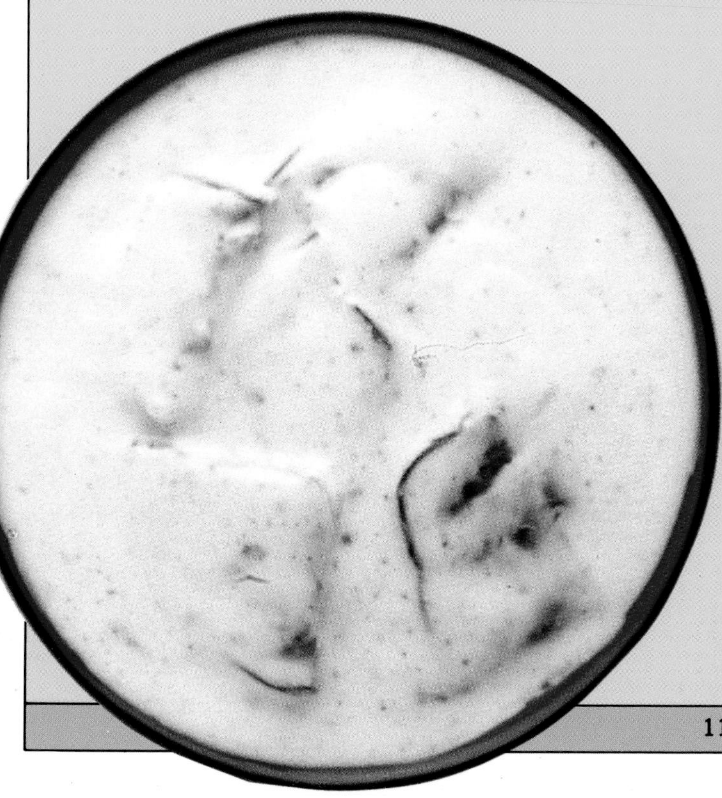

- 6-8 tbsp oil
- 1 small aubergine, cut into small pieces
- 12 fl oz / 325 ml / 1½ cups unsweetened yoghurt
- ½ tsp salt
- ½ tsp ground roasted cumin (see basic recipes)
- ½ tsp chilli powder

1 Heat the oil in a karai and fry the aubergine pieces until brown. Drain.

2 In the bowl whisk the yoghurt until smooth. Add the salt, cumin and chilli and mix thoroughly.

3 Place the fried aubergine pieces in a bowl and pour over the spiced yoghurt. Chill.

PUDINA CHUTNEY / MINT CHUTNEY

2 oz / 50 g / ½ cup mint leaves, washed
2 oz / 50 g / ¼ cup tamarind juice (see basic recipes)
2 tbsp onions, chopped
2 cloves garlic
¾ in / 2 cm root ginger
2-3 green chillis
½ tsp salt
½ tsp sugar

1 Blend all the ingredients together until you have a smooth paste. Serve with any fried foods. (Can be stored in an airtight jar in the refrigerator for one week).

DHANIYA CHUTNEY / CORIANDER CHUTNEY

3 oz / 75 g / ¾ cup coriander (cilantro) leaves
4 cloves garlic
3 tbsp desiccated coconut
2 green chillis
2-3 tbsp lemon juice
½ tsp salt
¼ tsp sugar

1 Chop the sprigs of coriander and throw away the roots and lower stalk.

2 Blend the coriander with all the other ingredients until you have a smooth paste. Serve with any fried foods. (Can be stored in an airtight jar in the refrigerator for one week).

IMLEEKI CHUTNEY / TAMARIND CHUTNEY

4 oz / 100 g / ½ cup tamarind
12 fl oz / 325 ml / 1½ cups hot water
¼ tsp chilli powder
1 tbsp lemon juice
2 tbsp brown sugar
¼ tsp salt

1 Soak the tamarind in the water for about 30 minutes. Squeeze the tamarind and strain.

2 Combine the tamarind juice with the other ingredients and chill.

TAMATAR KI CHUTNEY / TOMATO CHUTNEY

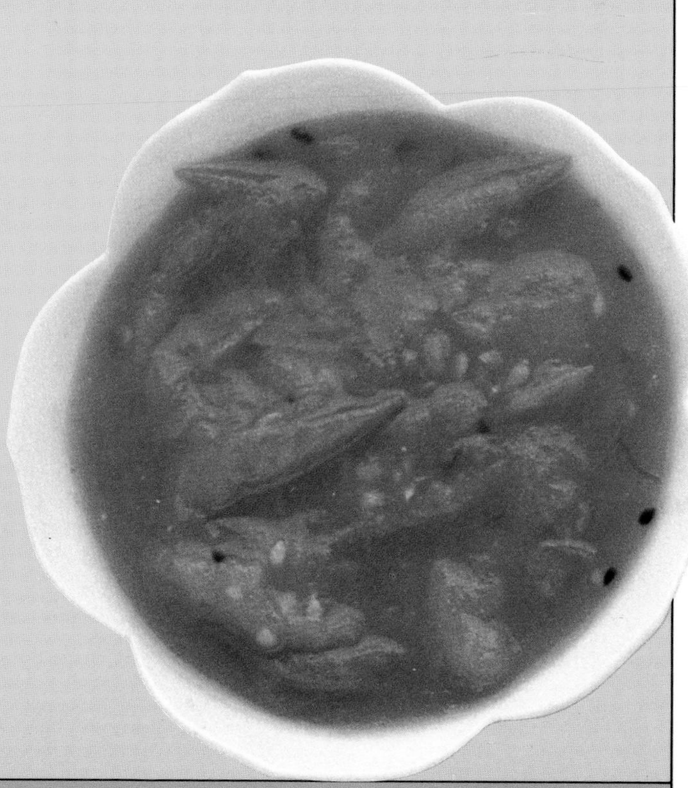

1 tbsp oil
½ tsp panch phoron
1 lb / 450 g / 1½ cups tomatoes, quartered
½ tbsp salt
1 tbsp sugar
1 tsp cornflour (cornstarch), mixed with a little milk

1 Heat the oil in a small saucepan over medium heat. Add the panch phoron and let them sizzle for a few seconds.

2 Add the tomatoes, cover and cook until the tomatoes are soft. Add the salt and sugar and cook a further 10 minutes.

3 Thicken with the cornflour mixture and remove from the heat. Chill.

ANARAS KI CHUTNEY / PINEAPPLE CHUTNEY

½ tbsp oil

½ tsp whole mustard seeds

8 oz / 237 g / 1 cup canned pineapple, crushed and drained

big pinch of salt

1 tsp cornflour (cornstarch) mixed with a little milk

1 Heat the oil in a small pan over medium heat. Add the mustard seeds and let them sizzle for a few seconds.

2 Add the drained pineapple and salt and, stirring occasionally; cook for about 10 minutes.

3 Thicken with the cornflour mixture and remove from the heat. Chill.

CACHUMBAR / TOMATO, CUCUMBER AND ONION RELISH

- 8 oz / 225 g / ¾ cup tomatoes, chopped into ¼ in / 0.5 cm pieces
- 8 oz / 225 g / 1 cup cucumber, cut into ¼ in / 0.5 cm pieces
- 4 oz / 100 g / ½ cup onions, chopped
- 2-3 green chillis
- ½ tsp salt
- ¼ tsp sugar
- 3 tbsp lemon juice
- 2 tbsp coriander leaves, chopped

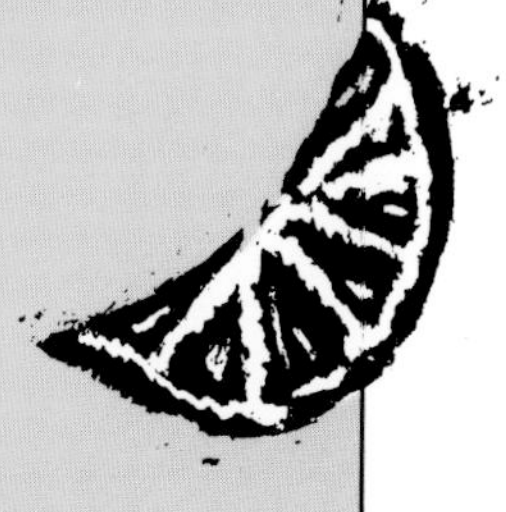

Mix all the ingredients together in a small bowl. Cover and set aside to chill. Serve with any Indian meal.

BASIC
RECIPES

IMLEE / TAMARIND JUICE

3 oz / 75 g / ½ cup dried tamarind
8 fl oz / 225 ml / 1 cup hot water

1 Soak the tamarind in the water for about 30 minutes.

2 Squeeze well to draw out all the pulp. Strain and use as required. (By adjusting the amount of water you can change the consistency).

ONION MIXTURE

2 large onions
3 tomatoes
1½ in / 3.5 cm root ginger
5 cloves garlic
3-4 green chillis
4 tsp white vinegar

Blend all the ingredients together until you have a smooth paste. Pour into an airtight bottle and keep in the refrigerator until needed. It will keep for up to two weeks.

DAHI / YOGHURT

2 pints / 1.15 litres / 5 cups milk

2½ tbsp yoghurt

1 Bring the milk to the boil, stirring constantly. Remove from the heat. Let it cool so that it just feels warm.

2 Place the yoghurt in a large bowl and whisk until smooth. Slowly add in the lukewarm milk and stir gently. Cover the bowl and leave in a warm place overnight. Chill.

ROASTED CUMIN

2 tbsp whole cumin seeds

1 Place the cumin seeds in a small pan over medium heat and dry roast them, stirring constantly. The seeds will turn a few shades darker. (Take care not to burn them).

2 Cool and grind. Store in a spice bottle until required. Coriander seeds and dried red chillis can be roasted and ground in a similar manner and stored.

PANIR / HOME MADE COTTAGE CHEESE

6 pints / 3.5 litres / 15 cups milk
7 fl oz / 200 ml / scant cup warm water
3 fl oz / 75 ml / ⅜ cup white vinegar

1 Bring the milk to boil, stirring constantly, over high heat. Remove from heat.

2 Combine the water and the vinegar.

3 Slowly add the vinegar solution to the boiled milk. As soon as the milk curdles do not add any more.

4 Put three to four layers of cheesecloth on a sieve and strain the curdled milk. Tie up the ends of the cheesecloth and squeeze out as much of the liquid as possible. Hang it up to drain thoroughly. Use in savoury and sweet dishes. Makes 21 oz / 575 g / approx. 3½ cups panir.

GARAM MASALA

3 tbsp cardamom seeds
3 × 1 in / 2.5 cm cinnamon sticks
½ tbsp cumin seeds
½ tsp black peppercorns
½ tsp cloves
¼ of a nutmeg

Grind all the spices together until they are finely ground. Store in a spice bottle until required. (The ingredients may be added in different proportions to suit individual tastes).

GHEE / CLARIFIED BUTTER

1 lb / 450 g unsalted butter

1 Heat the butter in a saucepan over low heat. Let it simmer for 15-20 minutes until all the white residue turns golden and settles at the bottom.

2 Remove from the heat, strain and cool.

3 Pour into an airtight bottle and store in a cool place.

Acknowledgements

I should like to thank my mother who gave me some recipes and helped in the preparation of food for photography; Maya Mami who also gave me some recipes along with much valuable advice; Rita Sen and Sheila Sengupta who sent recipes; Neyla Freeman for her constant encouragement; and Wendy Vincent who did most of the typing for the book. Thanks also go to Beagle Gallery of 303 Westbourne Grove, London W.11 and Ganesha of 6 Park Walk, London S.W.10 who kindly lent props for use in the photographs.

Sumana Ray

Appetisers

Deep fried semolina-cheese squares 15
Pakoras 17

Starches

Rice-peas cumin 82
(*) Rice coconut chiles 86
Rice with lentils - 88

BREADS

Paratha bread - 99
Whole wheat unleavened bread 98
Stuffed layered bread 93
Whole wheat puri 92
Yoghurt Bread - 94
Stuffed deep fried bread - 95
Nan 97
White bread - 86

Misc

Stuffed deep-fried eggs 27
Fried egg curry 29

Raita - Chutneys

* Yoghurt-chiles cucumber 114
tomato-cucumber-onion relish - 119

pineapple Date spread
can 50u. rolls.
20 oz crushed pineapple
1 lb pitted dates, - chop
3 tbs apple juice
cook down in skillet
until chunky - pasty

Vegetables

Potato pancakes-chiles, cilantro 21
Veg cutlets (beet, carrot, pot cabbage) 22
Curried kidney beans - 39
Cabbage with coconut - 45
Cabbage with peas - 47
Okra with yoghurt - 52
Green beans - coconut
Eggplant - tomato chiles - 61
Whole small potato curry 67
Potatoes green pepper coconut 68
Cauliflower + potato curry 69
(*) Roasted Cauliflower 72
Cauliflower-potatoes-peas - 73
(*) veg in yoghurt + coconut sauce 77

Desserts

Semolina Halva - 103